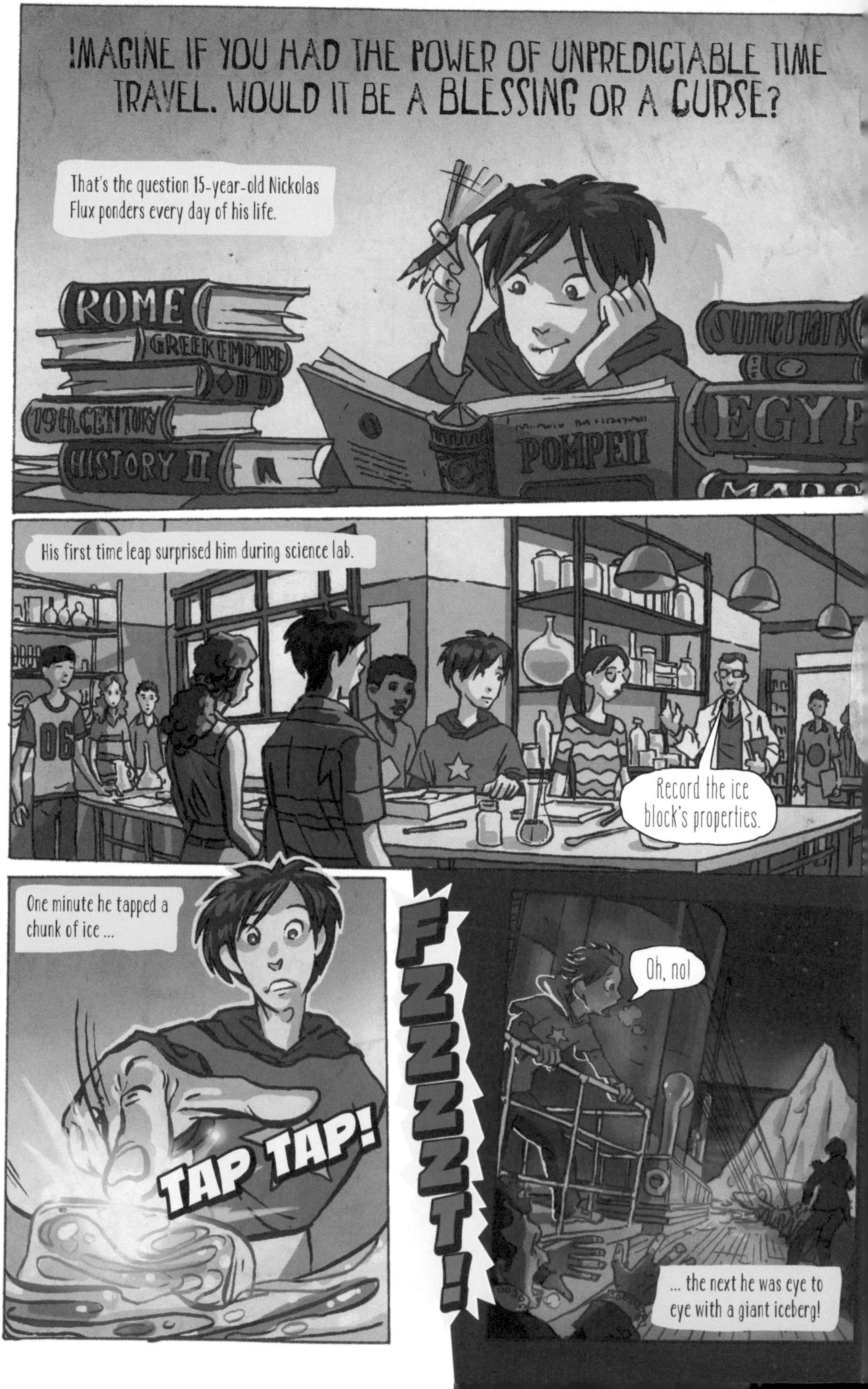
IMAGINE IF YOU HAD THE POWER OF UNPREDICTABLE TIME TRAVEL. WOULD IT BE A BLESSING OR A CURSE?
That's the question 15-year-old Nickolas Flux ponders every day of his life.
ROME
GREEK EMPIRE
19th.CENTURY
HISTORY II
POMPEII
Sumerians
His first time leap surprised him during science lab.
Record the ice block's properties.
One minute he tapped a chunk of ice ...
TAP TAP!
FZZZZT!
Oh, no!
... the next he was eye to eye with a giant iceberg!

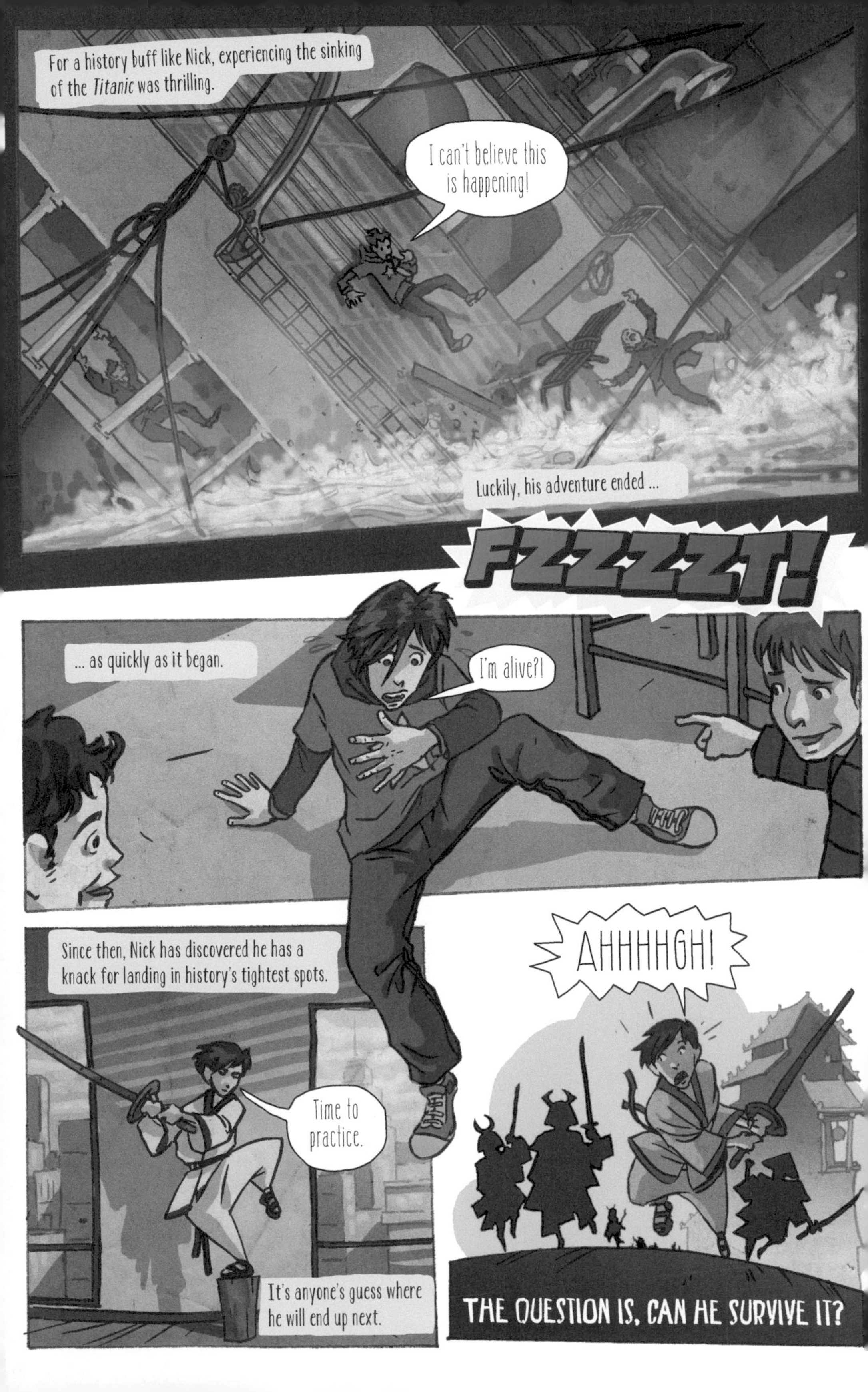
For a history buff like Nick, experiencing the sinking of the *Titanic* was thrilling.
I can't believe this is happening!
Luckily, his adventure ended ...
FZZZZT!
... as quickly as it began.
I'm alive?!
Since then, Nick has discovered he has a knack for landing in history's tightest spots.
Time to practice.
It's anyone's guess where he will end up next.
AHHHHGH!
THE QUESTION IS, CAN HE SURVIVE IT?

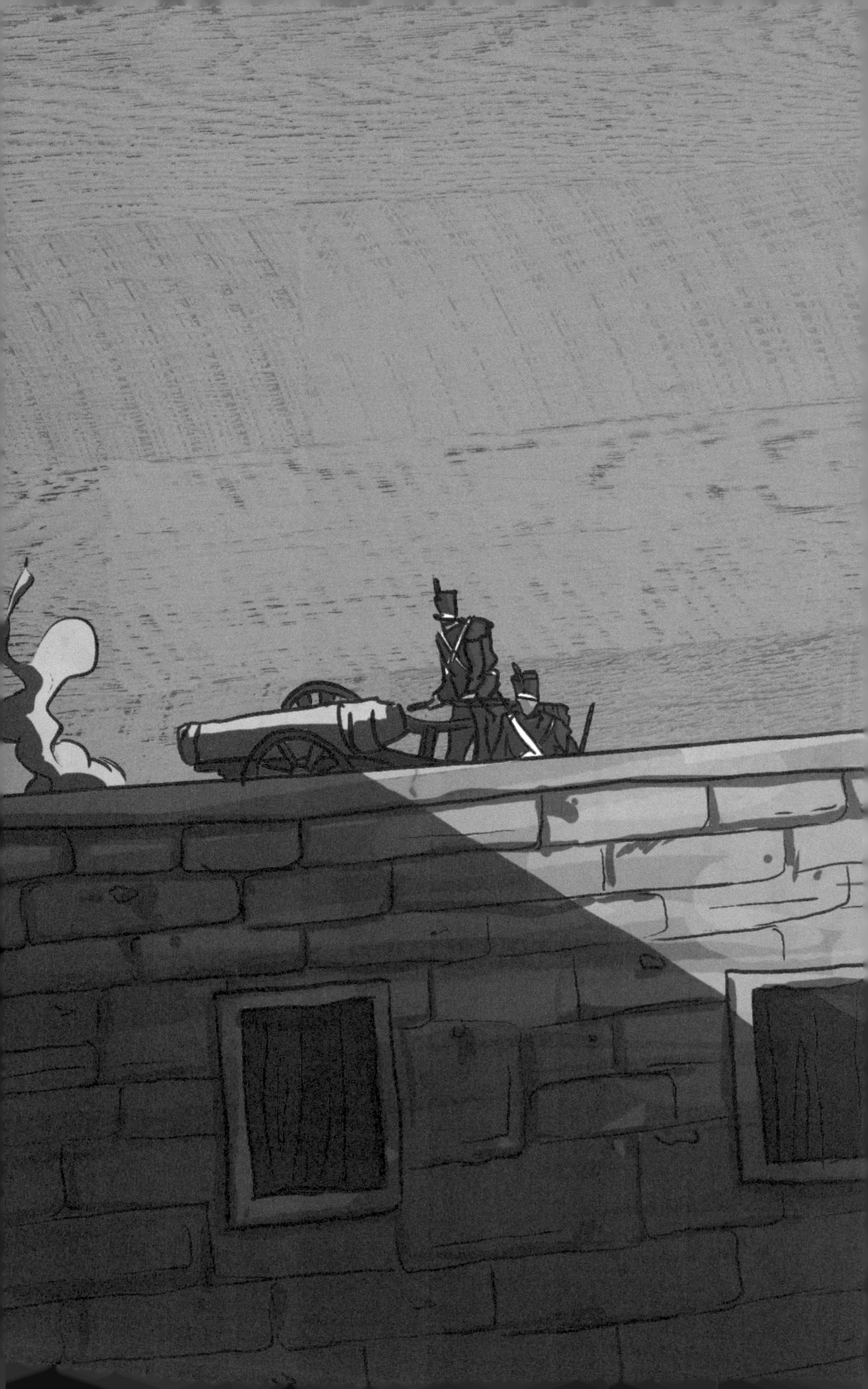

Nickolas Flux HISTORY CHRONICLES

DEFEND UNTIL DEATH!

NICKOLAS FLUX and the Battle of the Alamo

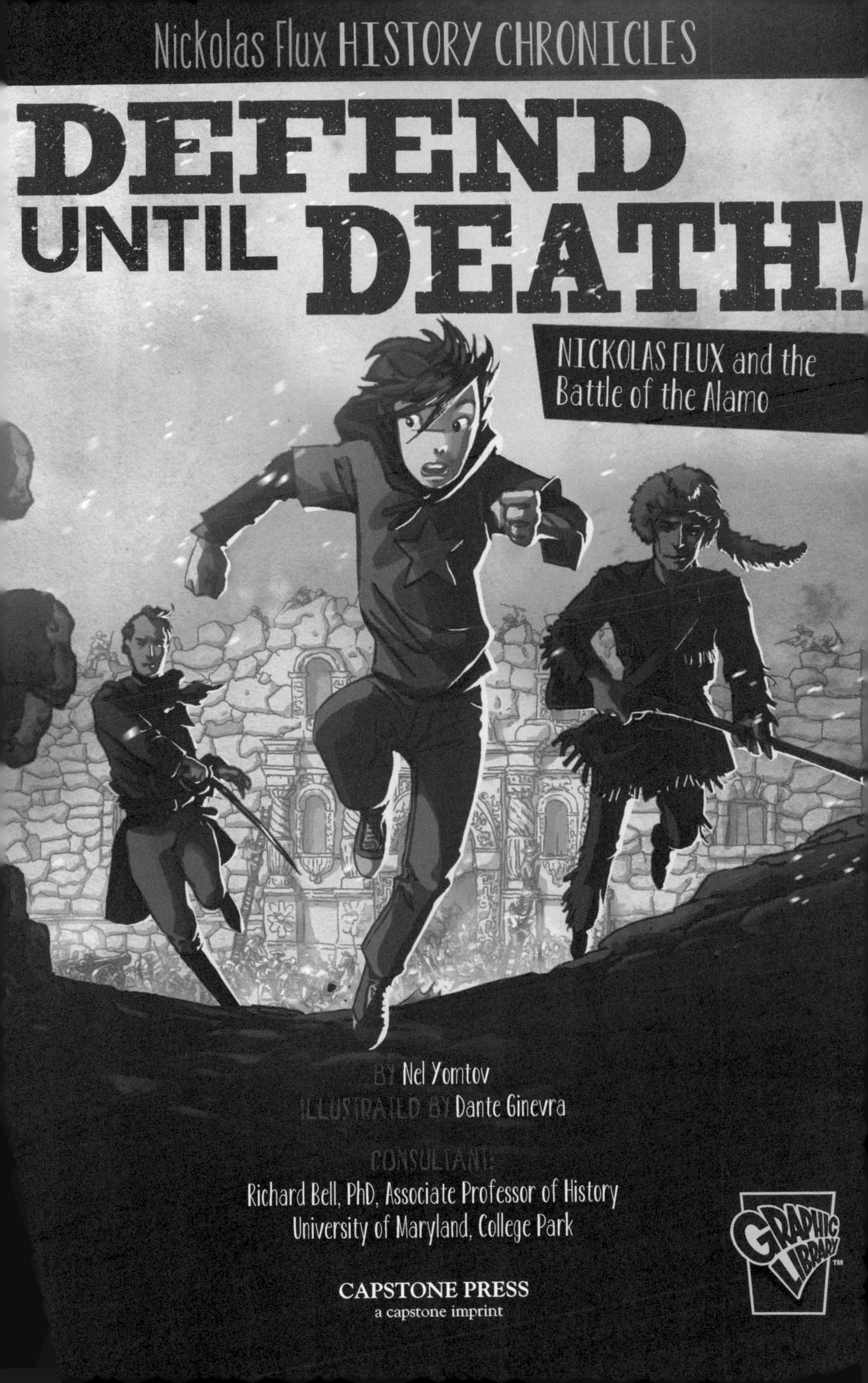

BY Nel Yomtov

ILLUSTRATED BY Dante Ginevra

CONSULTANT:
Richard Bell, PhD, Associate Professor of History
University of Maryland, College Park

CAPSTONE PRESS
a capstone imprint

Graphic Library is published by Capstone Press,
1710 Roe Crest Drive, North Mankato, Minnesota 56003
www.capstonepub.com

Library of Congress Cataloging-in-Publication Data
Yomtov, Nelson.
  Defend until death! : Nickolas Flux and the Battle of the Alamo / by
Nel Yomtov ; illustrated by Dante Ginevra.
      pages cm.—(Graphic library. Nickolas Flux history chronicles)
  Summary: "In graphic novel format, follows the adventures of
Nickolas Flux as he travels back in time and must survive the Battle
of the Alamo"—Provided by publisher.
  Includes bibliographical references and index.
  ISBN 978-1-4765-3945-4 (library binding)
  ISBN 978-1-4765-5149-4 (paperback)
  ISBN 978-1-4765-6006-9 (eBook PDF)
1. Alamo (San Antonio, Tex.)—Juvenile literature. 2. Alamo (San An-
tonio, Tex.)—Siege, 1836—Juvenile literature. 3. Texas—History—To
1846—Juvenile literature. 4. San Antonio (Tex.)—Buildings, structures,
etc.—Juvenile literature. 5. Alamo (San Antonio, Tex.)—Comic books,
strips, etc. 6. Alamo (San Antonio, Tex.)—Siege, 1836—Comic books,
strips, etc. 7. Texas—History—To 1846—Comic books, strips, etc. 8.
San Antonio (Tex.)—Buildings, structures, etc.—Comic books, strips, etc.
I. Ginevra, Dante, 1976– illustrator. II. Title.
  F390.Y66 2014
  976.4'03—dc23   2013028000

Photo Credits:
Design Elements: Shutterstock (backgrounds)

Editor's note:
A direct quotation appears on the following page:
Page 17 (letter), from a letter by William Travis dated February 24,
1836, taken from the Texas State Library and Archives Commission
(http://www.tsl.state.tx.us/treasures/republic/alamo/travis-about.html).

EDITOR
Christopher L. Harbo

DESIGNER
Ashlee Suker

ART DIRECTOR
Nathan Gassman

PRODUCTION SPECIALIST
Kathy McColley

Printed in the United States   5605

TABLE OF CONTENTS

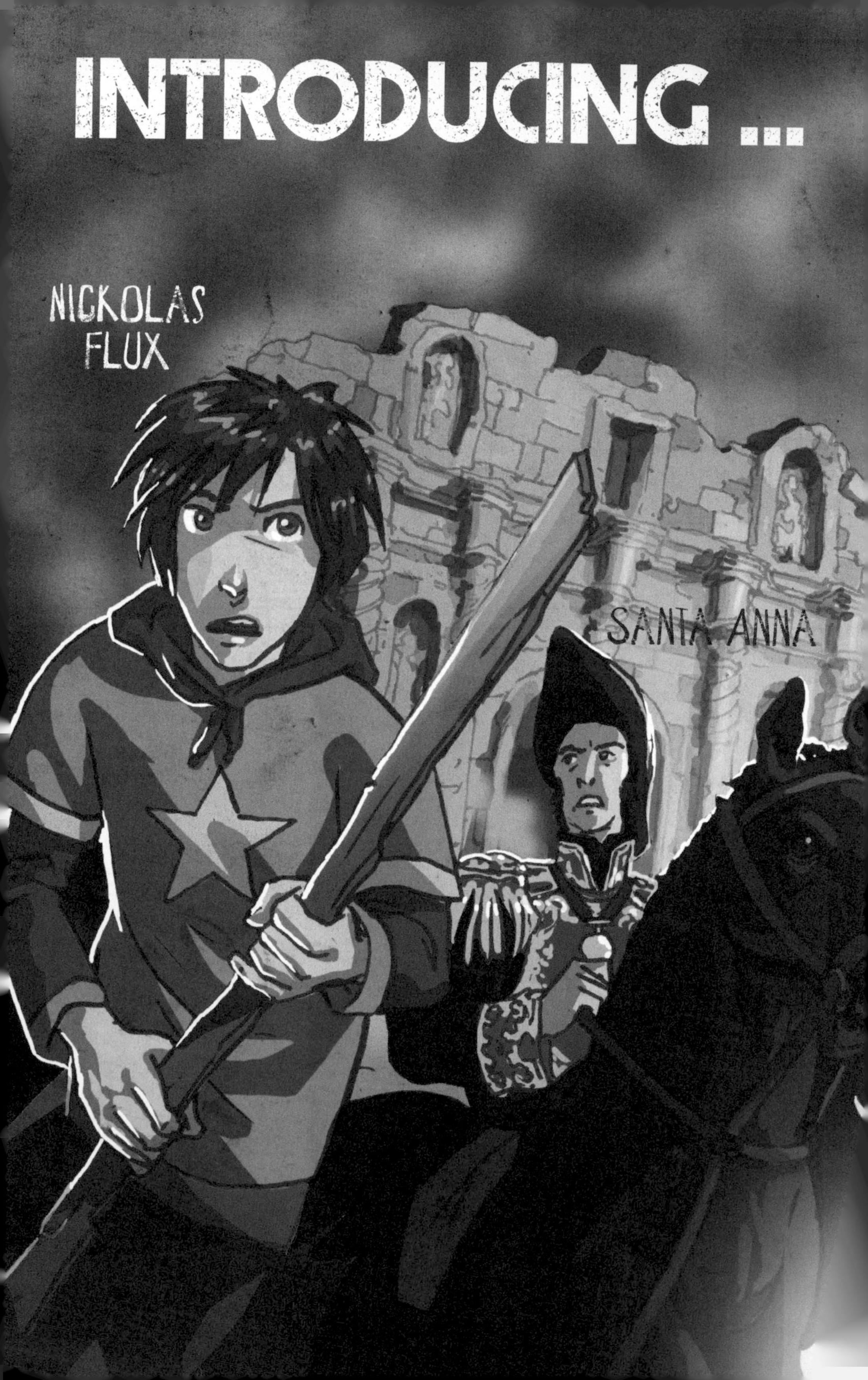
INTRODUCING ...
NICKOLAS FLUX
SANTA ANNA

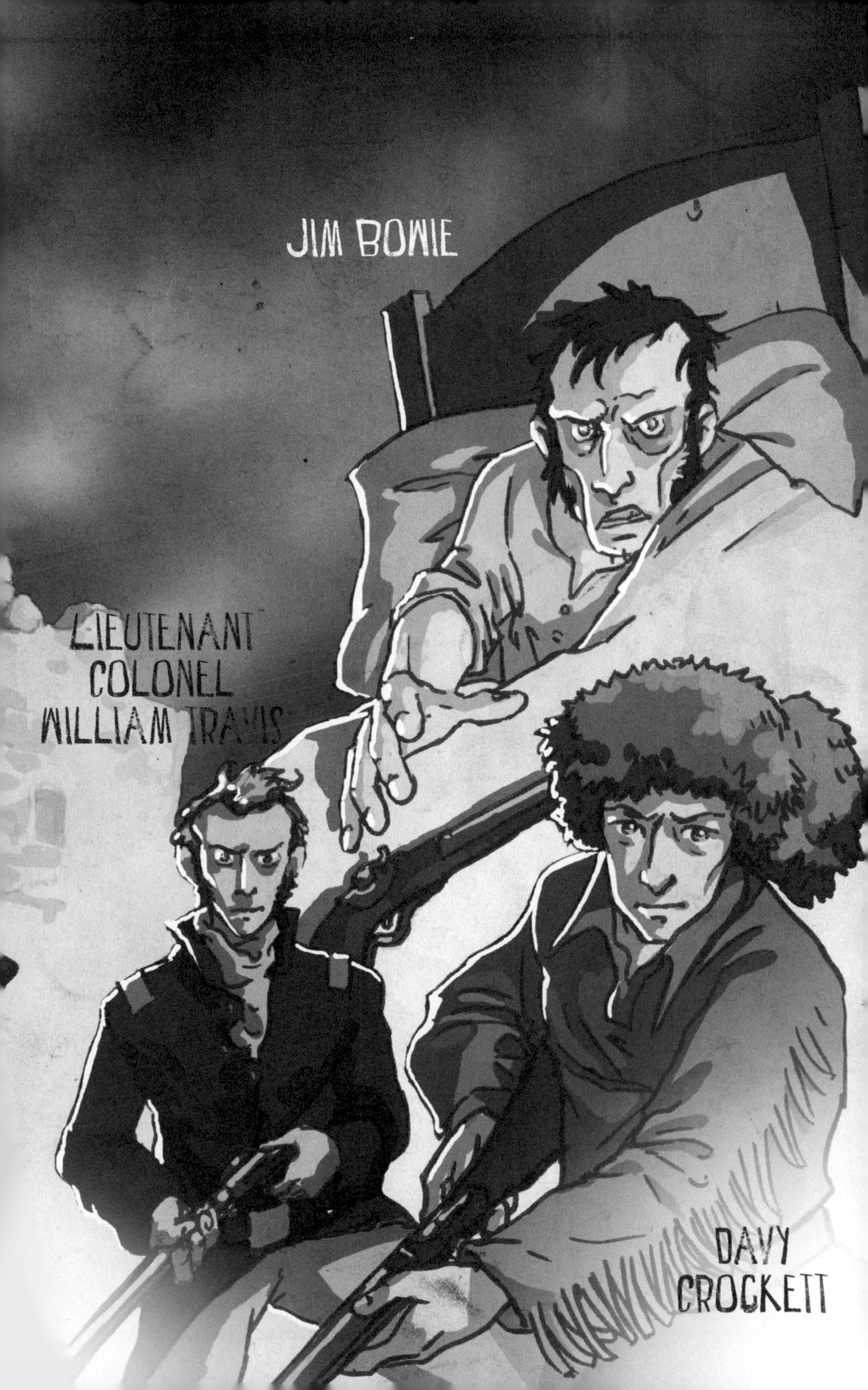
JIM BOWIE
LIEUTENANT COLONEL WILLIAM TRAVIS
DAVY CROCKETT

CHAPTER ONE

BATTLE ON THE GRIDIRON

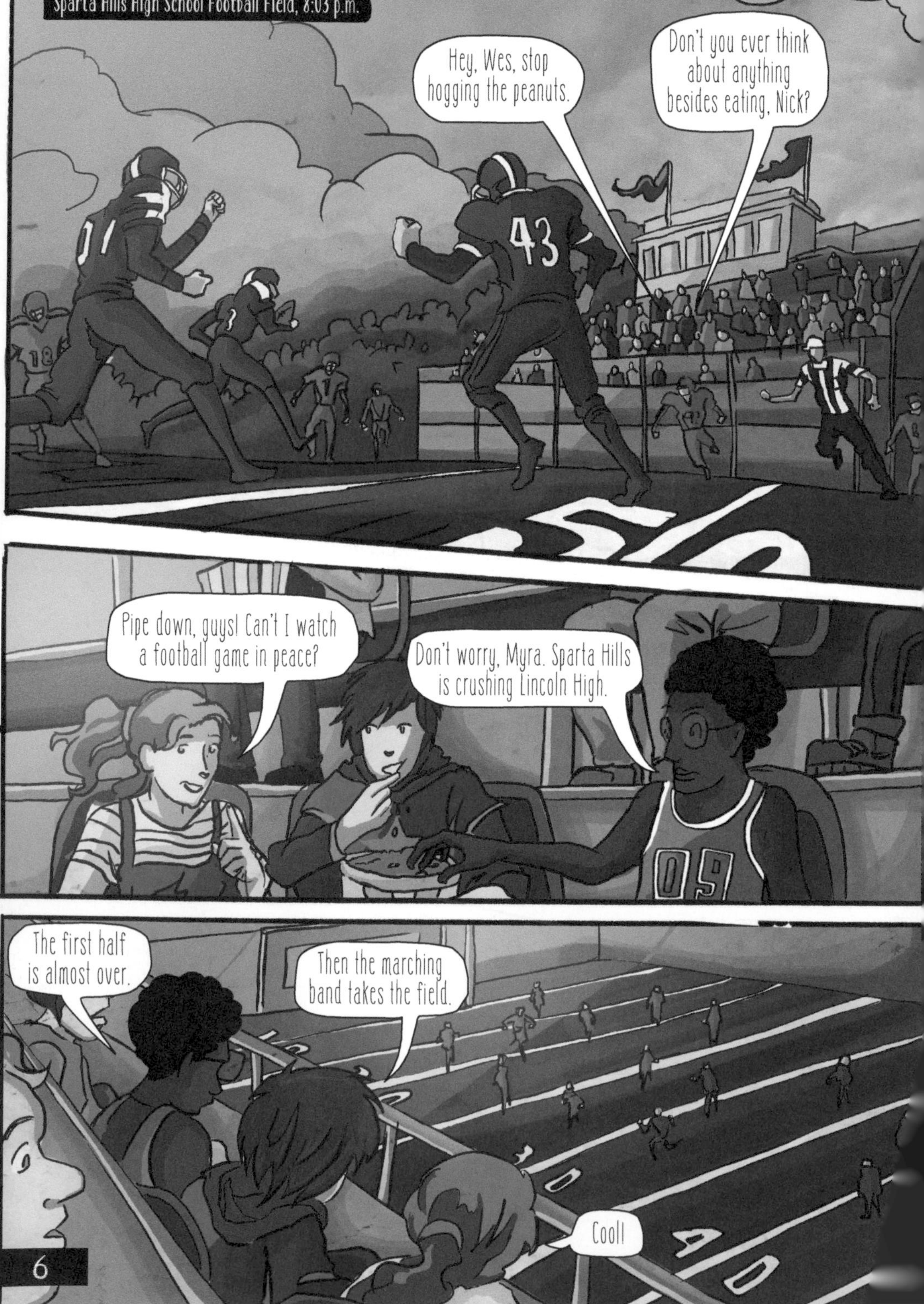
Sparta Hills High School Football Field, 8:03 p.m.
Hey, Wes, stop hogging the peanuts.
Don't you ever think about anything besides eating, Nick?
Pipe down, guys! Can't I watch a football game in peace?
Don't worry, Myra. Sparta Hills is crushing Lincoln High.
The first half is almost over.
Then the marching band takes the field.
Cool!

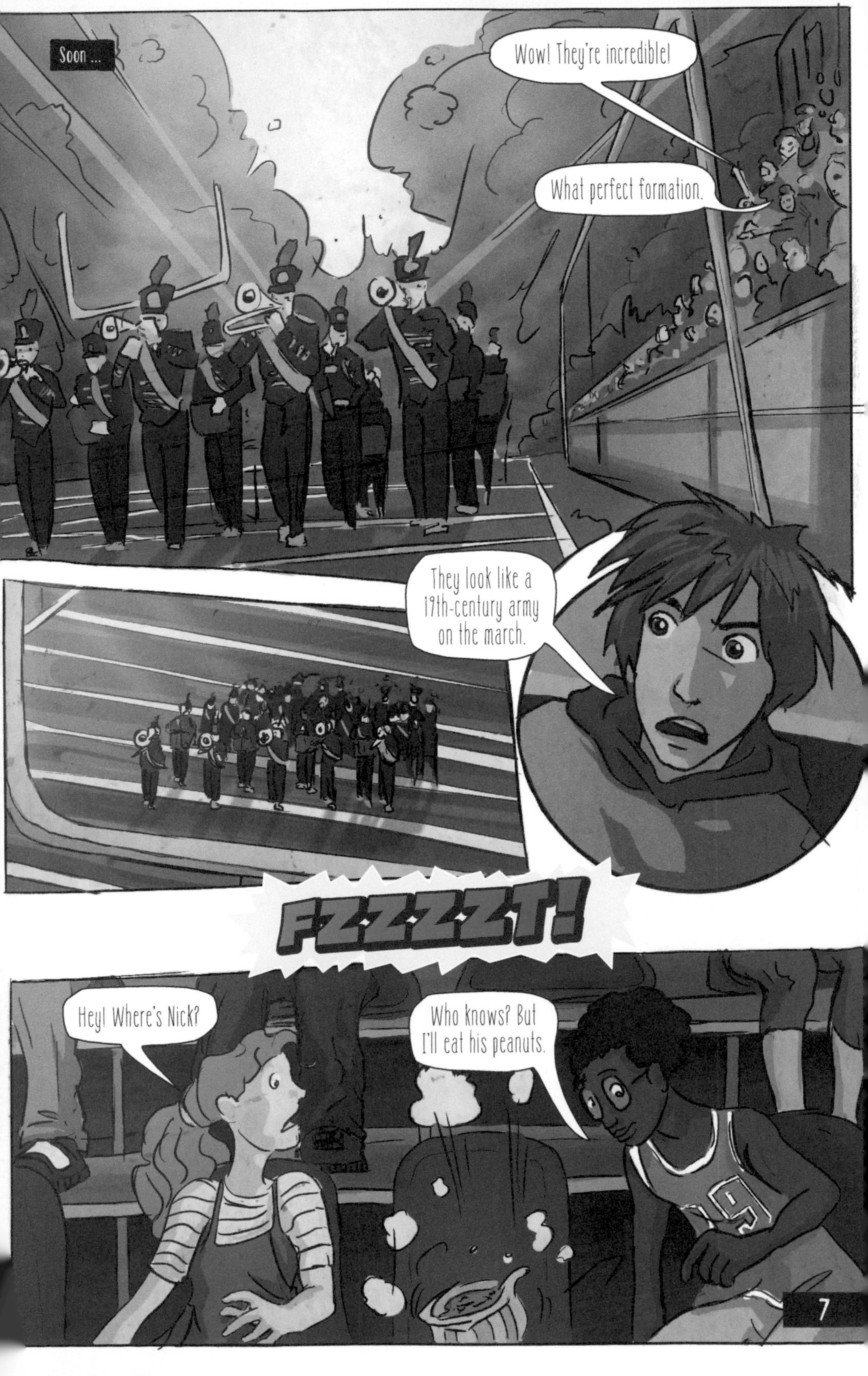
Soon ...
Wow! They're incredible!
What perfect formation.
They look like a 19th-century army on the march.
FZZZZT!
Hey! Where's Nick?
Who knows? But I'll eat his peanuts.

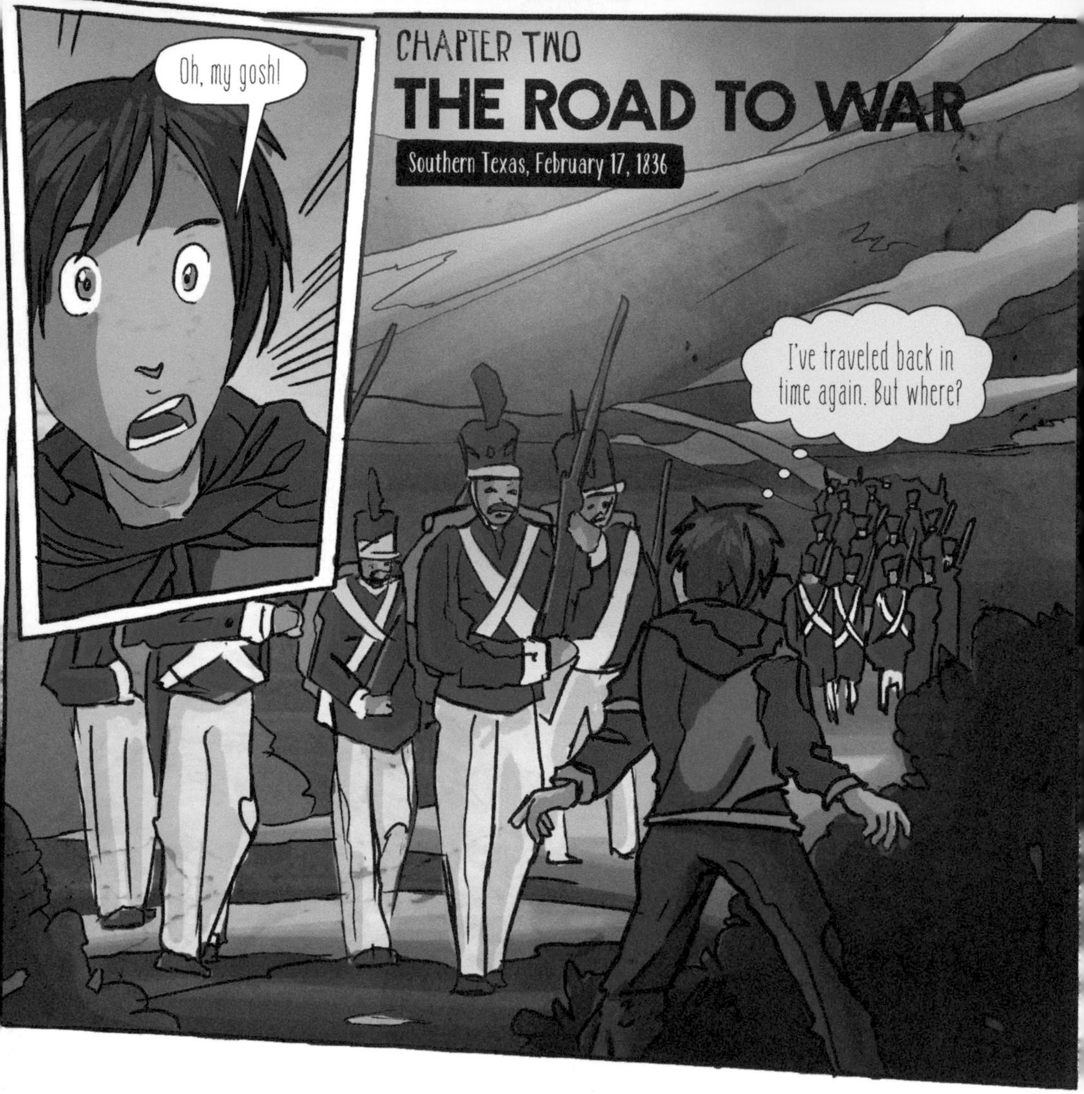
CHAPTER TWO
THE ROAD TO WAR
Southern Texas, February 17, 1836
Oh, my gosh!
I've traveled back in time again. But where?

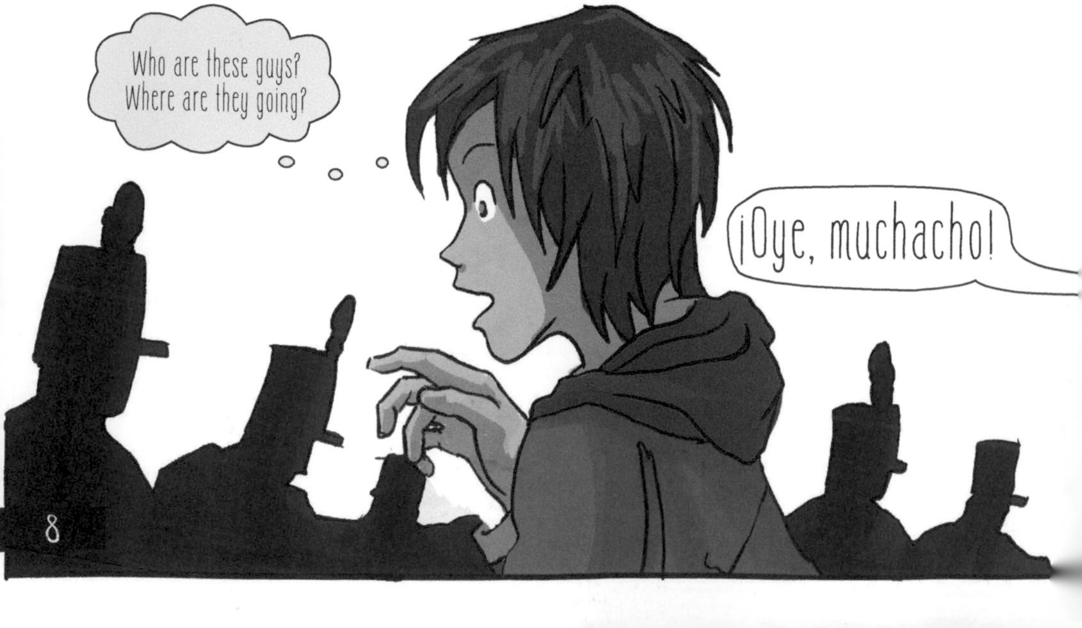
Who are these guys? Where are they going?
¡Oye, muchacho!

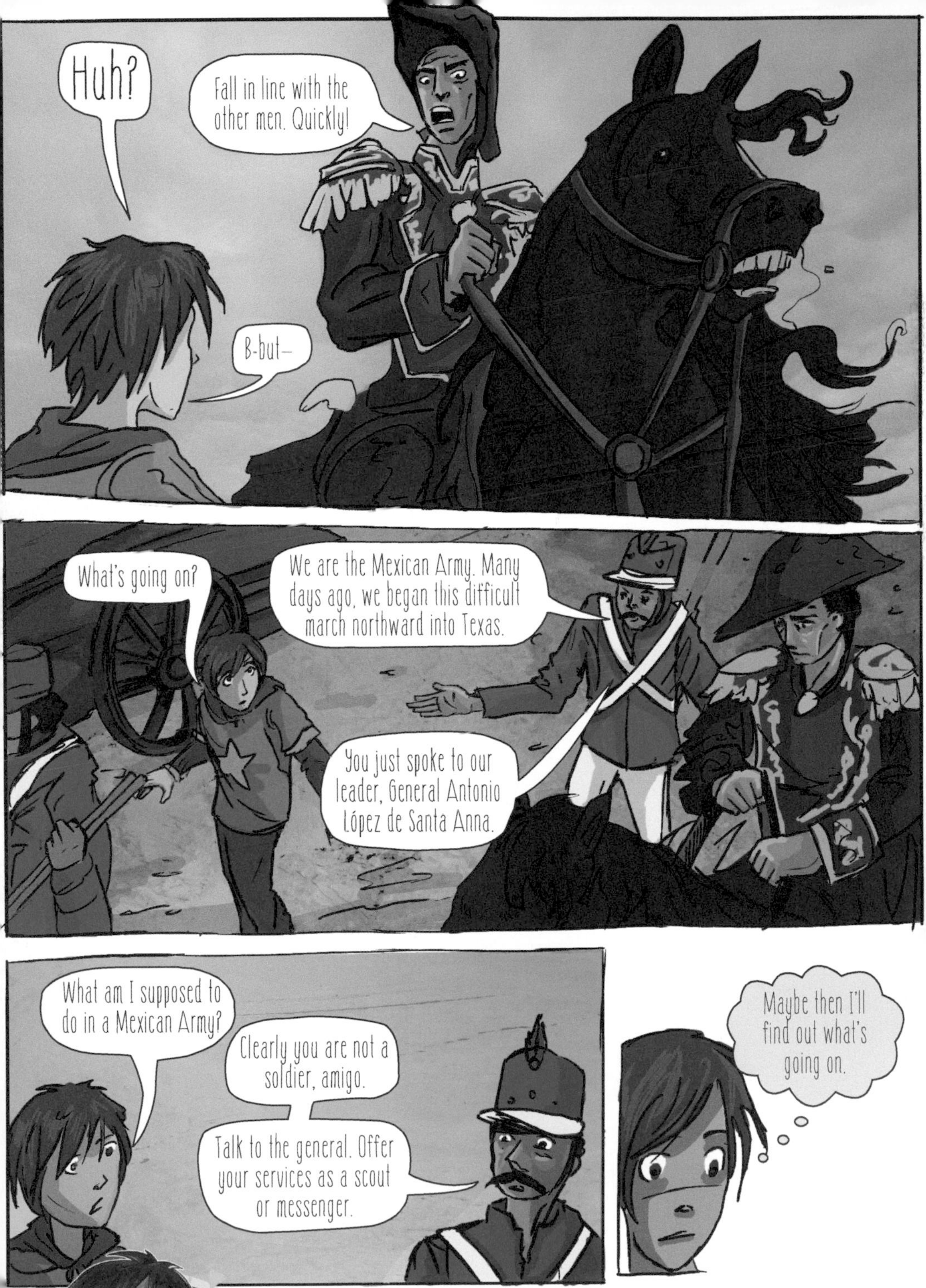
Huh?
Fall in line with the other men. Quickly!
B-but–
What's going on?
We are the Mexican Army. Many days ago, we began this difficult march northward into Texas.
You just spoke to our leader, General Antonio López de Santa Anna.
What am I supposed to do in a Mexican Army?
Clearly you are not a soldier, amigo.
Talk to the general. Offer your services as a scout or messenger.
Maybe then I'll find out what's going on.

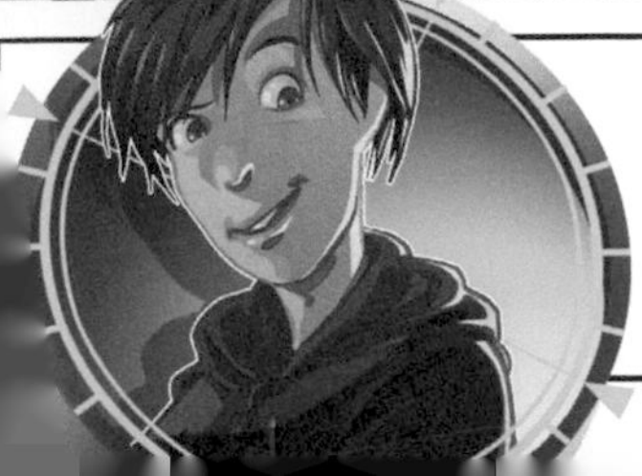

FLUX FACT

Santa Anna's march included more than 4,000 men, 21 field cannon, 1,800 mules, and hundreds of wagons loaded with food and supplies.

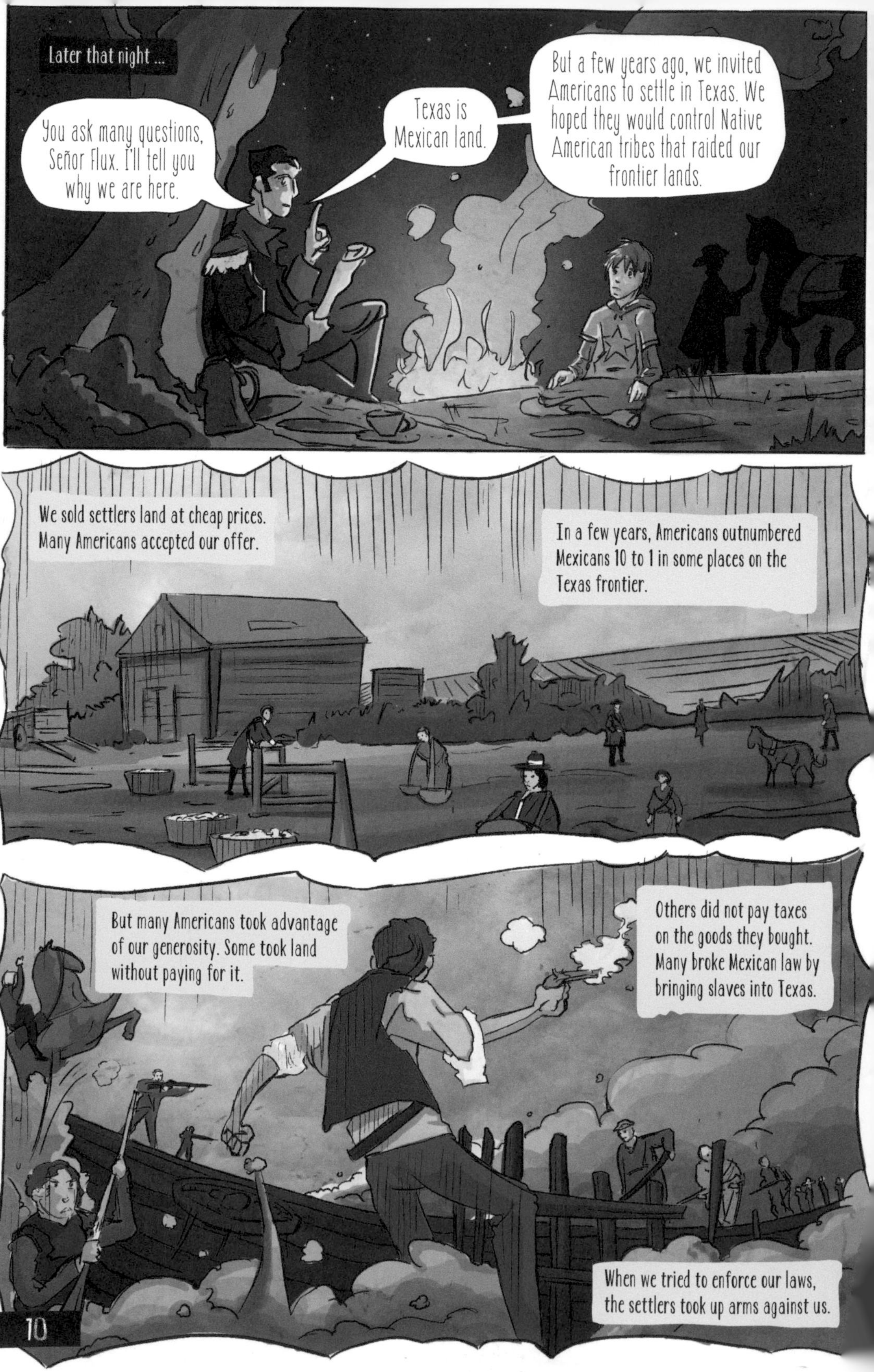
Later that night ...
You ask many questions, Señor Flux. I'll tell you why we are here.
Texas is Mexican land.
But a few years ago, we invited Americans to settle in Texas. We hoped they would control Native American tribes that raided our frontier lands.
We sold settlers land at cheap prices. Many Americans accepted our offer.
In a few years, Americans outnumbered Mexicans 10 to 1 in some places on the Texas frontier.
But many Americans took advantage of our generosity. Some took land without paying for it.
Others did not pay taxes on the goods they bought. Many broke Mexican law by bringing slaves into Texas.
When we tried to enforce our laws, the settlers took up arms against us.

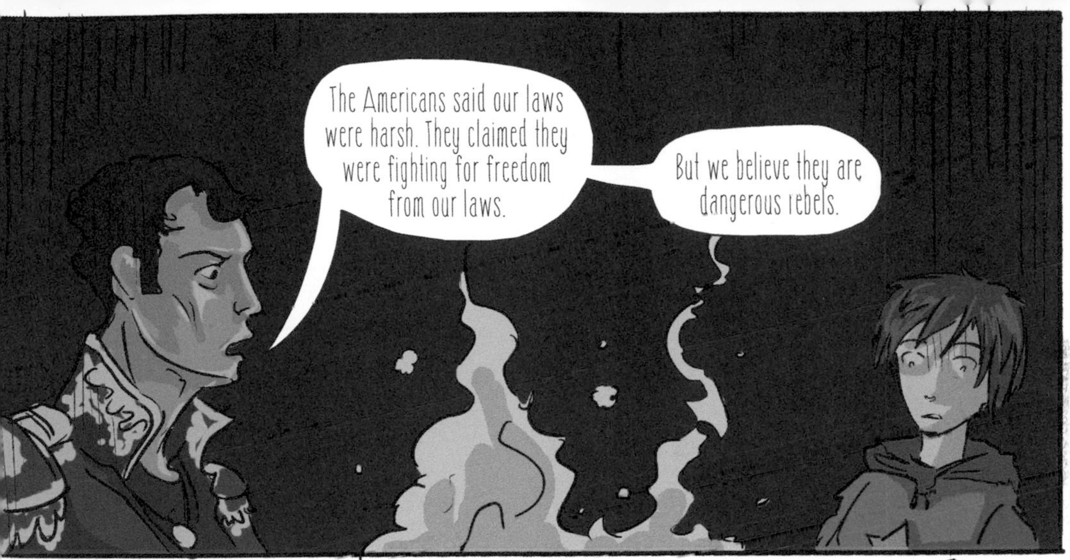

The Americans said our laws were harsh. They claimed they were fighting for freedom from our laws.
But we believe they are dangerous rebels.

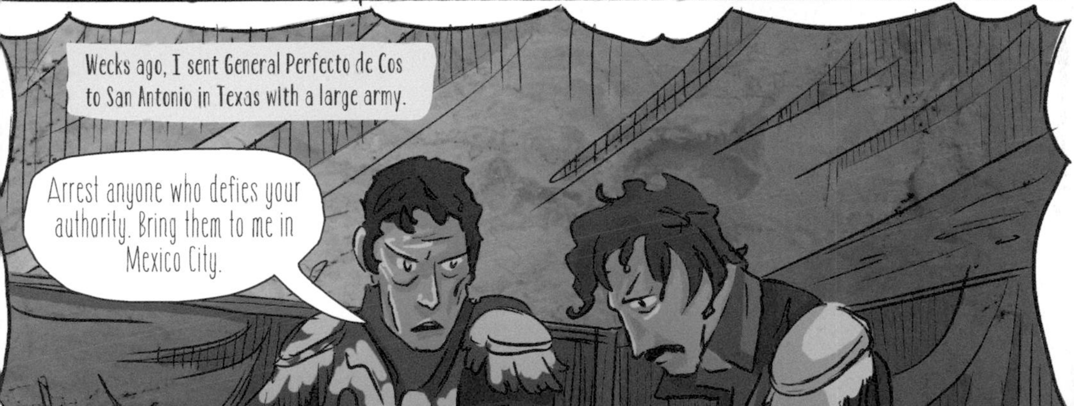

Weeks ago, I sent General Perfecto de Cos to San Antonio in Texas with a large army.
Arrest anyone who defies your authority. Bring them to me in Mexico City.

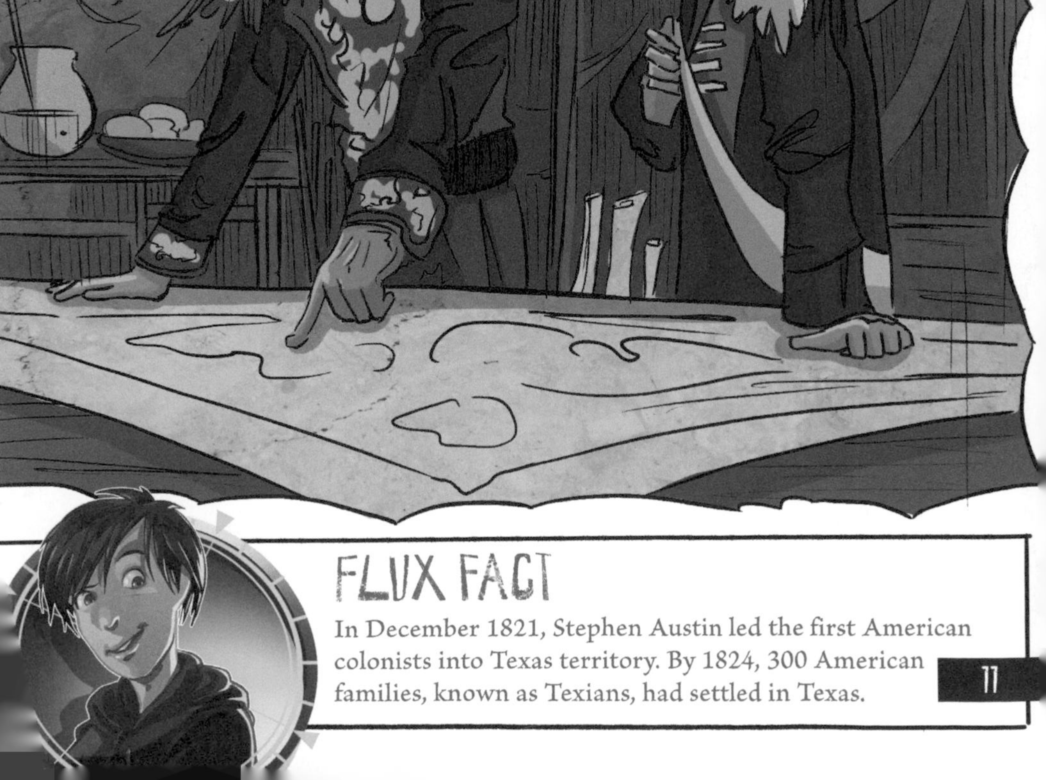

FLUX FACT

In December 1821, Stephen Austin led the first American colonists into Texas territory. By 1824, 300 American families, known as Texians, had settled in Texas.

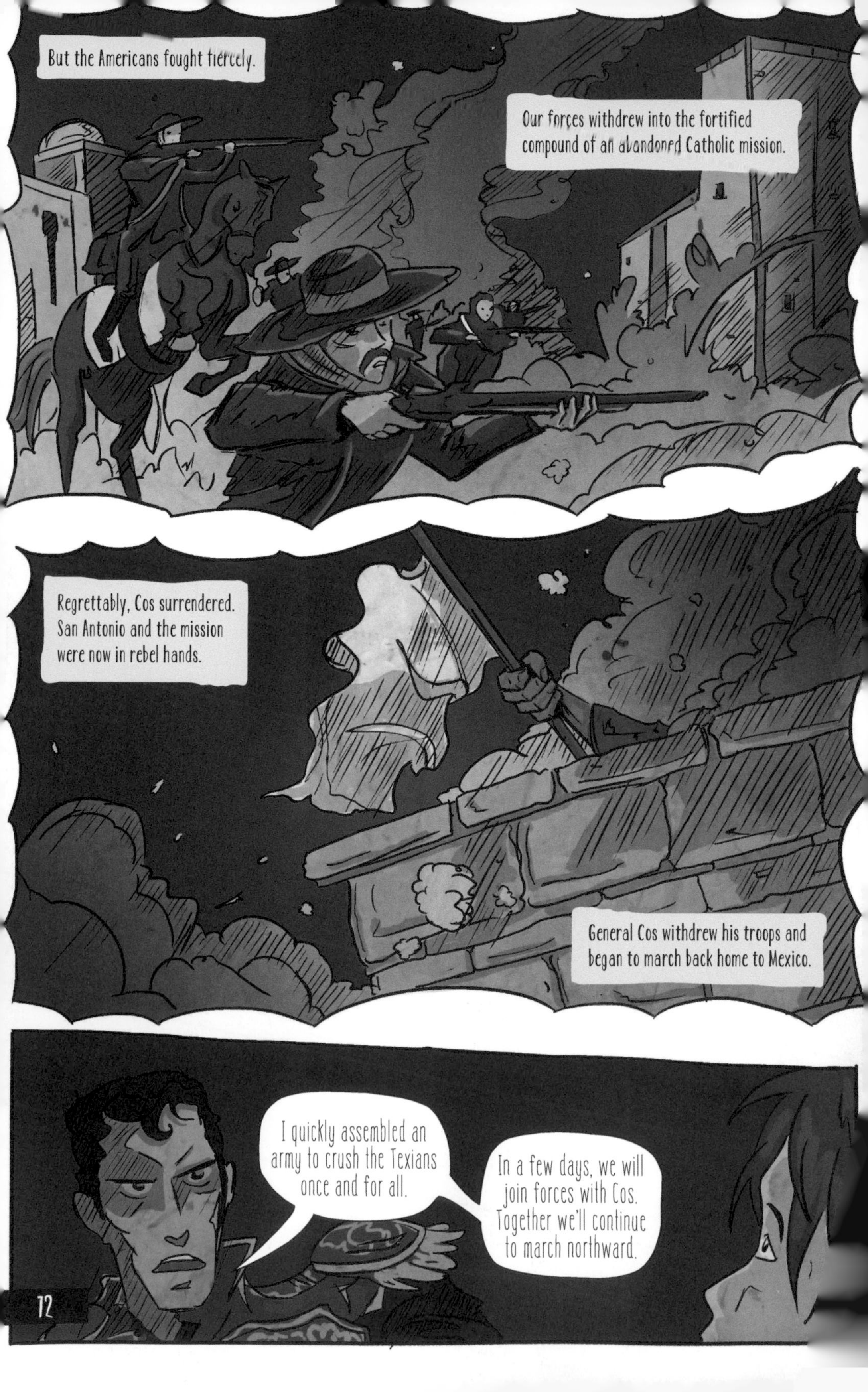

But the Americans fought fiercely.
Our forces withdrew into the fortified compound of an abandoned Catholic mission.
Regrettably, Cos surrendered. San Antonio and the mission were now in rebel hands.
General Cos withdrew his troops and began to march back home to Mexico.
I quickly assembled an army to crush the Texians once and for all.
In a few days, we will join forces with Cos. Together we'll continue to march northward.

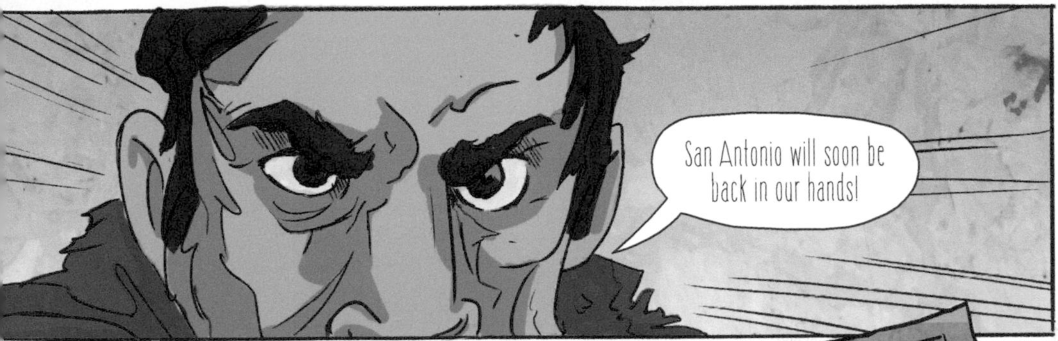
San Antonio will soon be back in our hands!

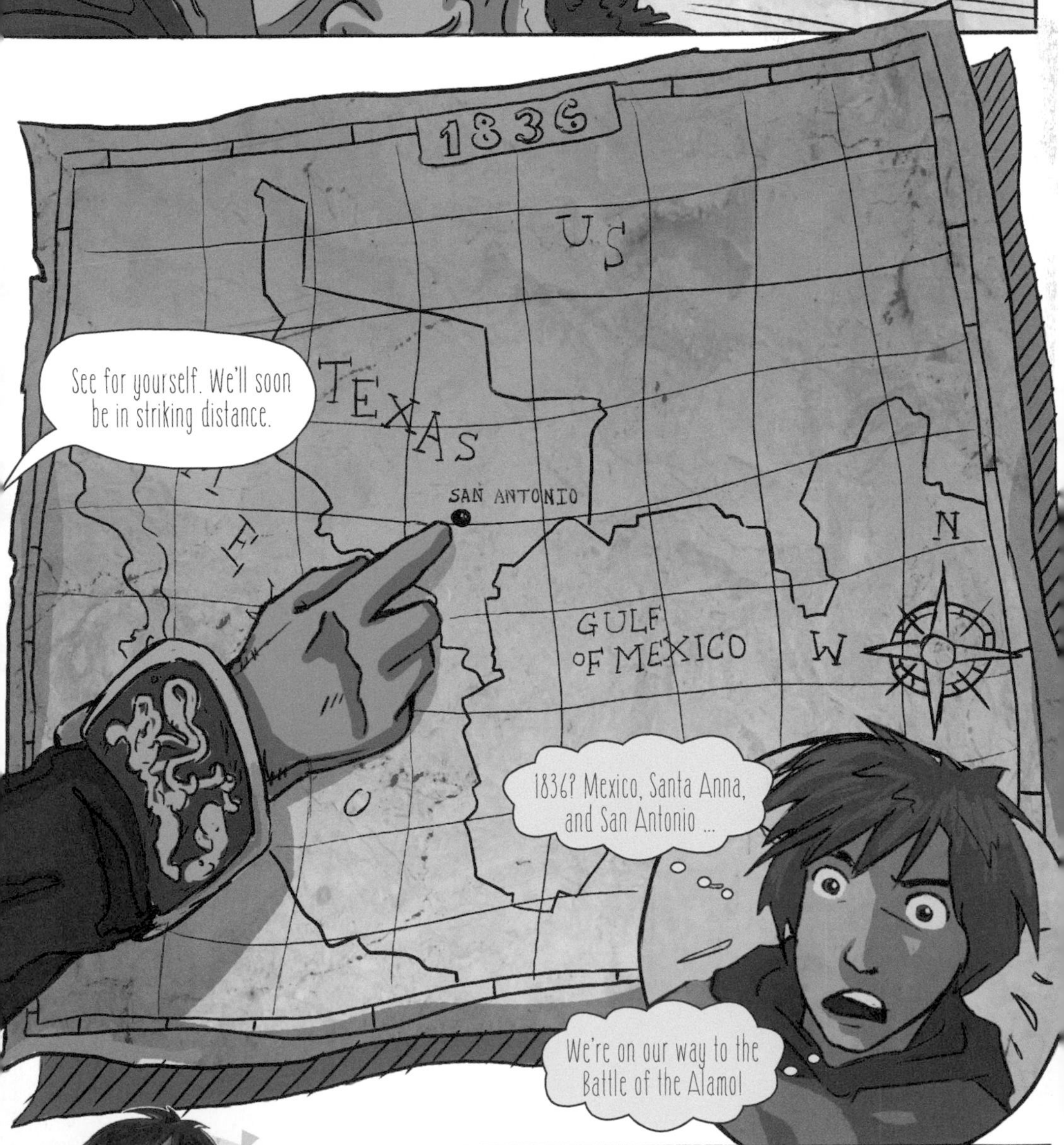
1836
US
TEXAS
SAN ANTONIO
GULF OF MEXICO
N
W
See for yourself. We'll soon be in striking distance.
1836? Mexico, Santa Anna, and San Antonio ...
We're on our way to the Battle of the Alamo!

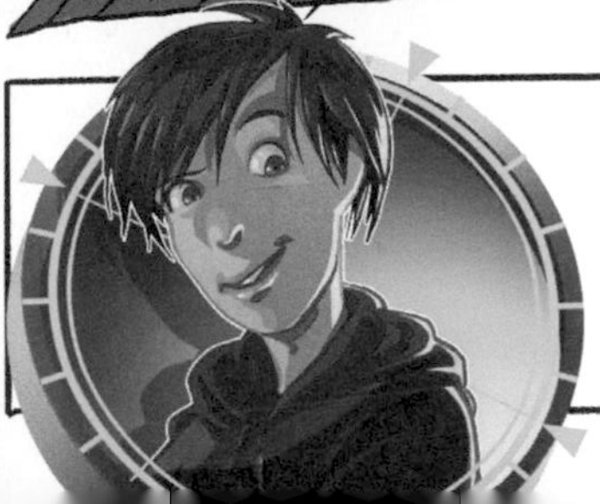

FLUX FACT

Antonio López de Santa Anna served as president of Mexico 11 times between 1833 and 1855. He was overthrown each time.

CHAPTER THREE
PREPARING TO FIGHT

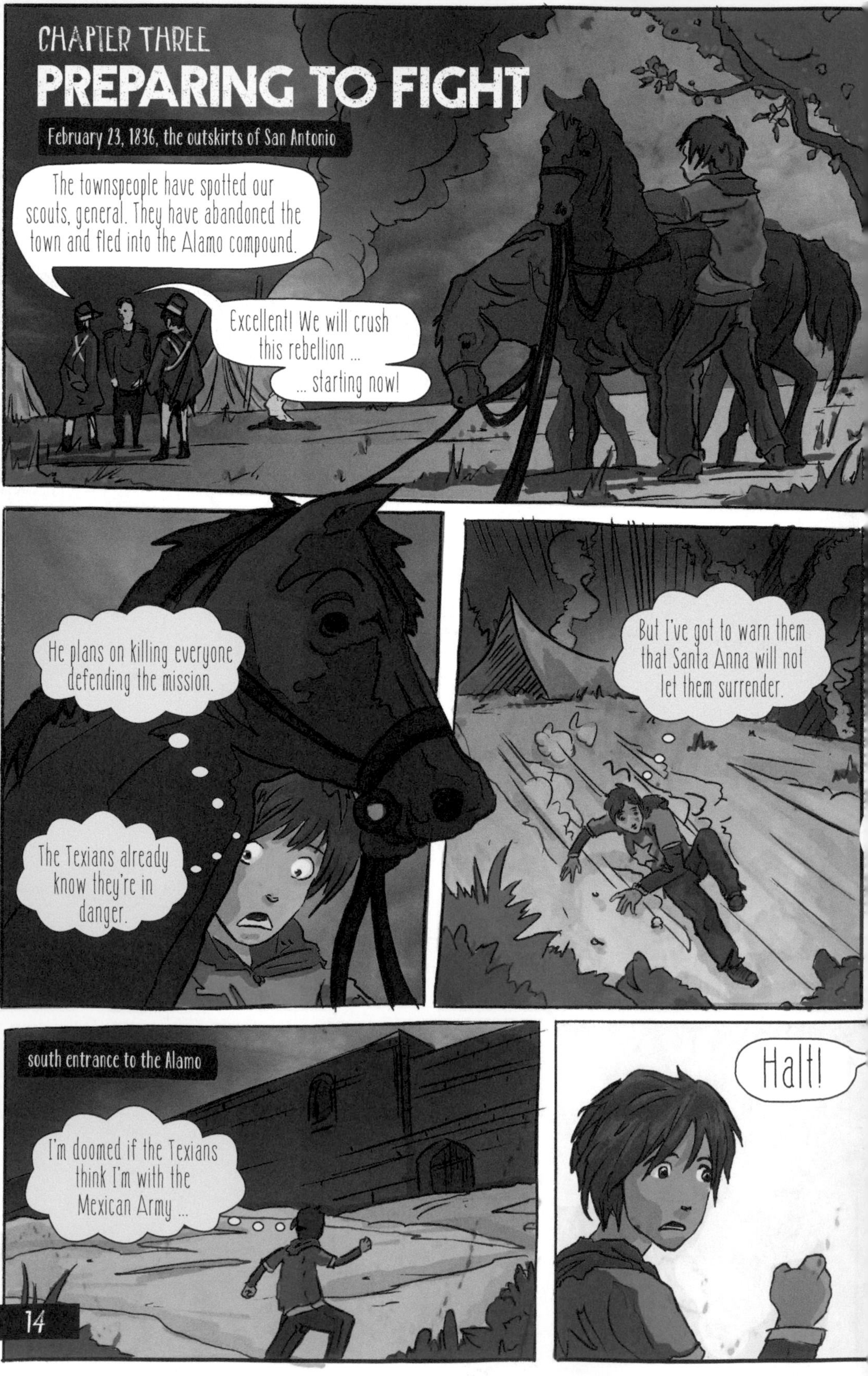
February 23, 1836, the outskirts of San Antonio
The townspeople have spotted our scouts, general. They have abandoned the town and fled into the Alamo compound.
Excellent! We will crush this rebellion ...
... starting now!
He plans on killing everyone defending the mission.
The Texians already know they're in danger.
But I've got to warn them that Santa Anna will not let them surrender.
south entrance to the Alamo
I'm doomed if the Texians think I'm with the Mexican Army ...
Halt!

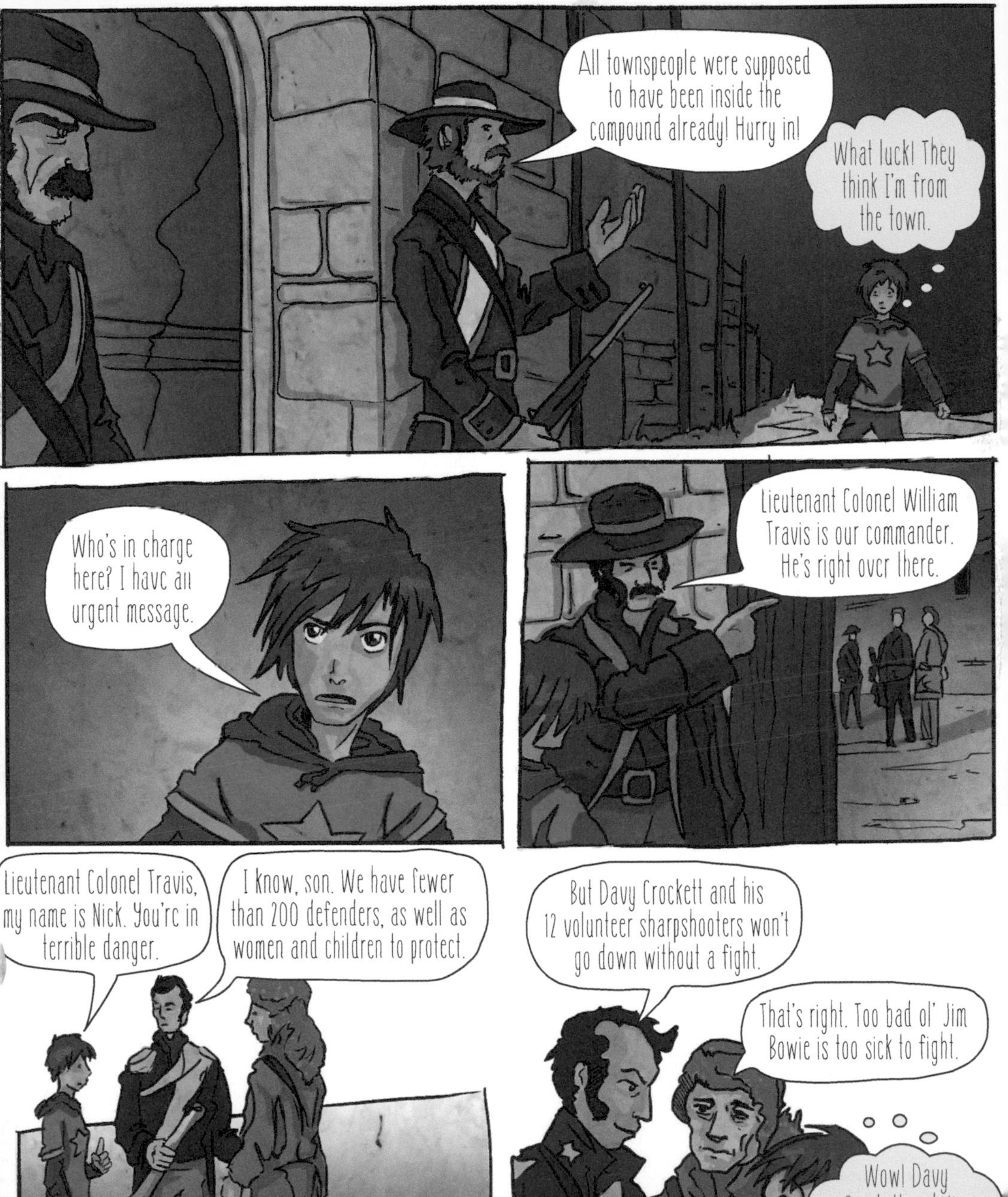
All townspeople were supposed to have been inside the compound already! Hurry in!
What luck! They think I'm from the town.
Who's in charge here? I have an urgent message.
Lieutenant Colonel William Travis is our commander. He's right over there.
Lieutenant Colonel Travis, my name is Nick. You're in terrible danger.
I know, son. We have fewer than 200 defenders, as well as women and children to protect.
But Davy Crockett and his 12 volunteer sharpshooters won't go down without a fight.
That's right. Too bad ol' Jim Bowie is too sick to fight.
Wow! Davy Crockett and Jim Bowie—legends of the American frontier!

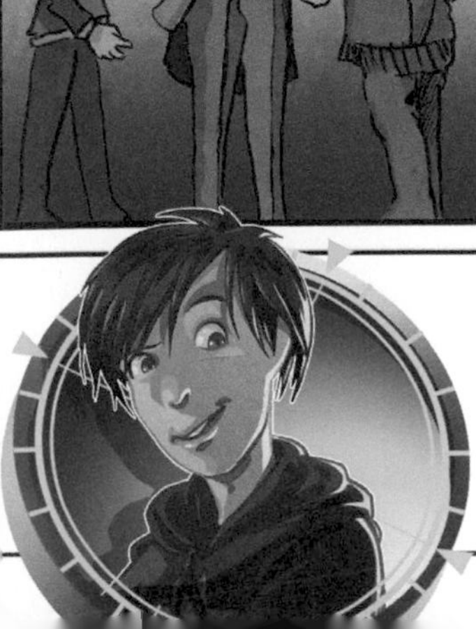

FLUX FACT

Jim Bowie was an American soldier and pioneer known for the large knife he carried. He came to the Alamo to fight. But a serious illness kept him in bed in the low barracks.

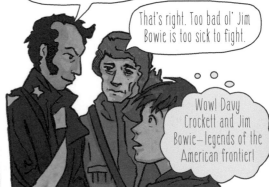

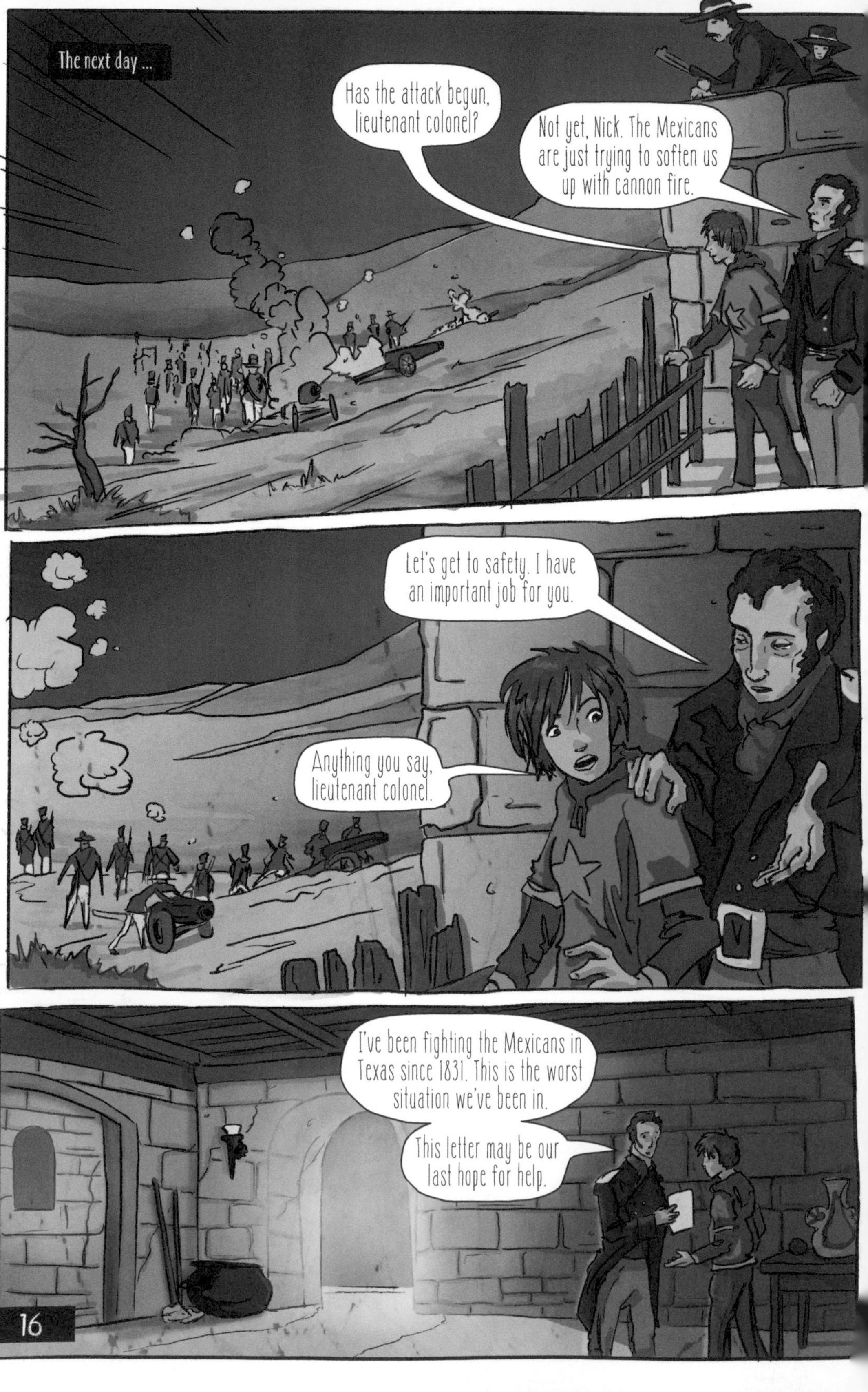
The next day ...
Has the attack begun, lieutenant colonel?
Not yet, Nick. The Mexicans are just trying to soften us up with cannon fire.
Let's get to safety. I have an important job for you.
Anything you say, lieutenant colonel.
I've been fighting the Mexicans in Texas since 1831. This is the worst situation we've been in.
This letter may be our last hope for help.

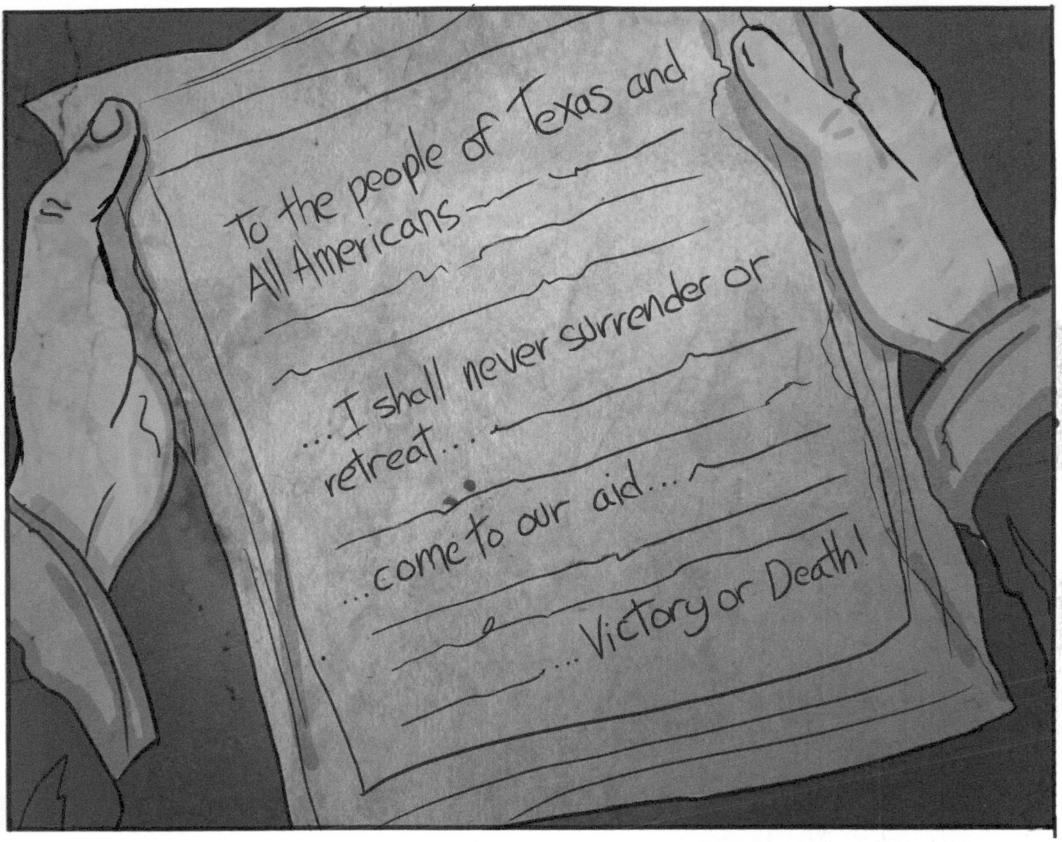
To the people of Texas and All Americans
...I shall never surrender or retreat...
...come to our aid...
...Victory or Death!

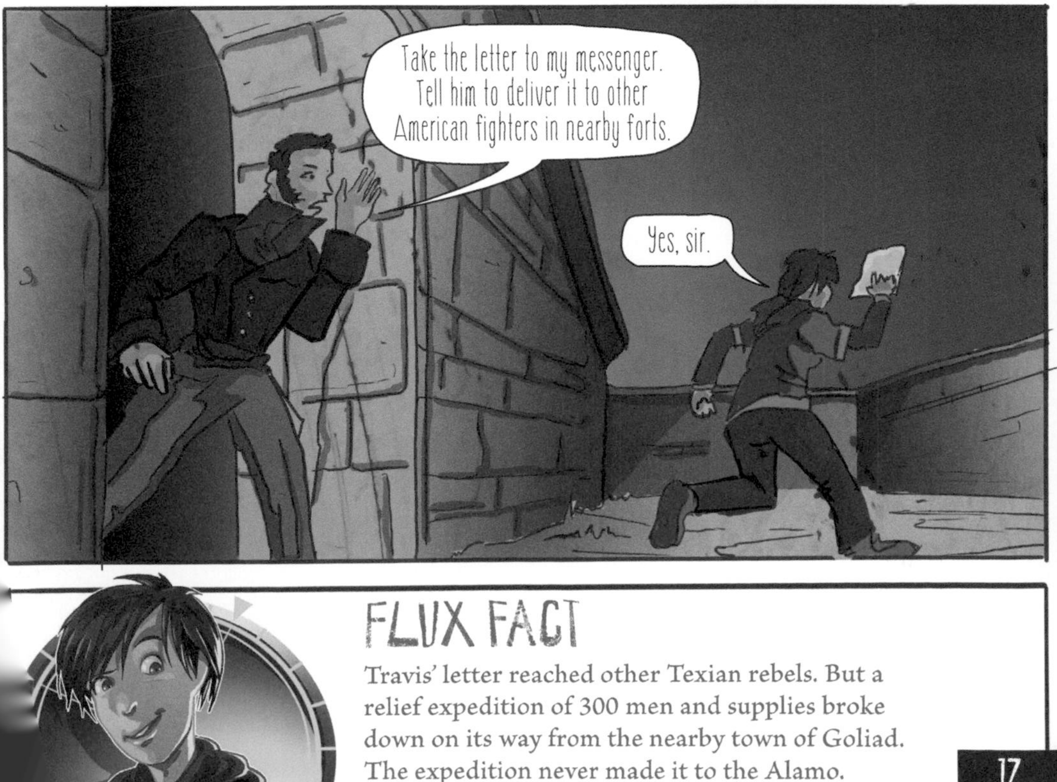
Take the letter to my messenger. Tell him to deliver it to other American fighters in nearby forts.
Yes, sir.

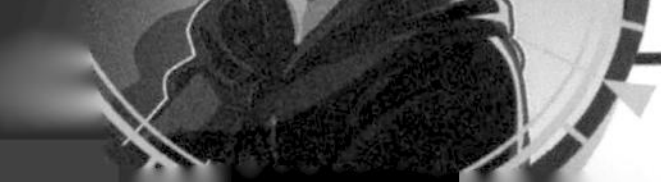

FLUX FACT

Travis' letter reached other Texian rebels. But a relief expedition of 300 men and supplies broke down on its way from the nearby town of Goliad. The expedition never made it to the Alamo.

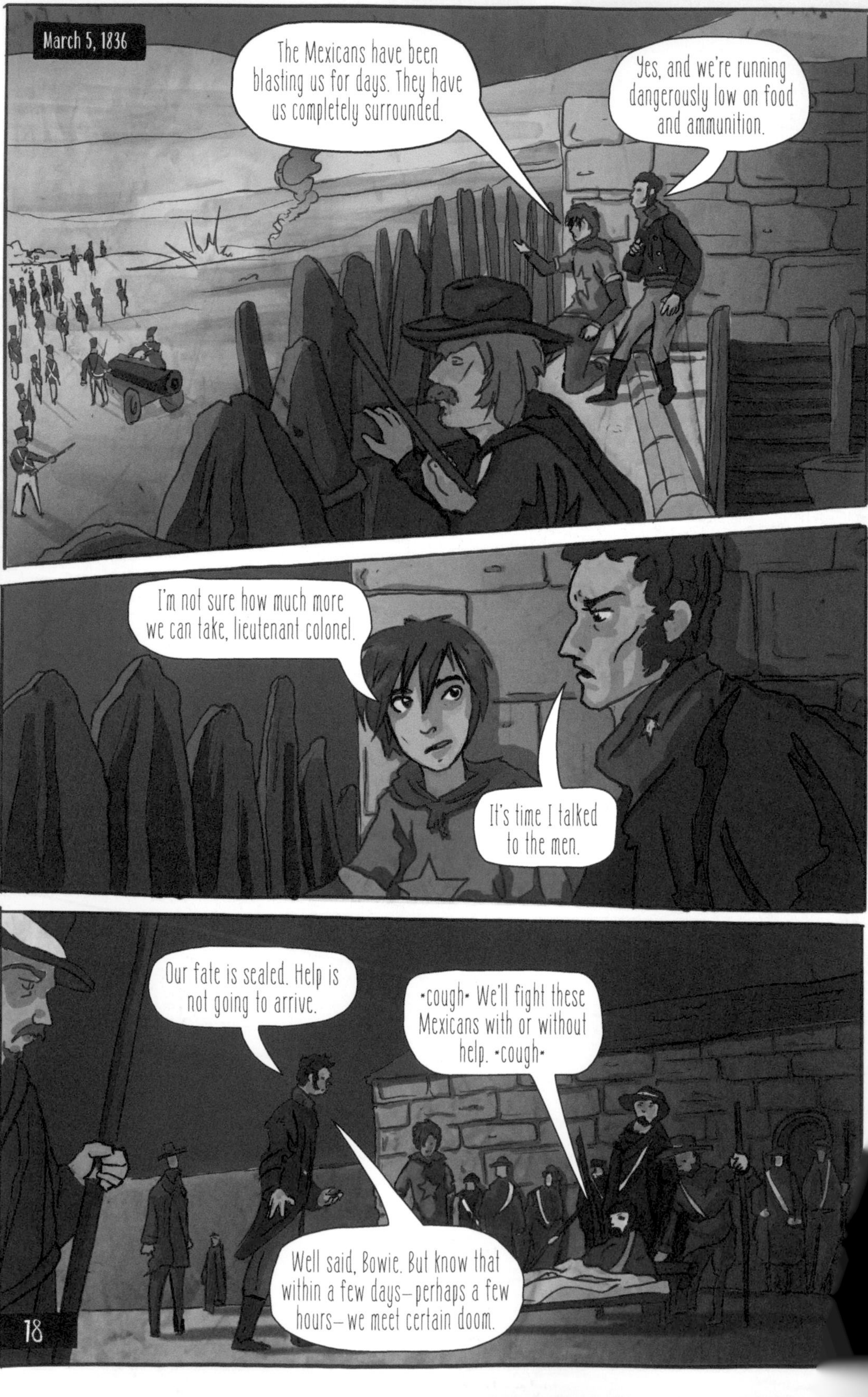
March 5, 1836
The Mexicans have been blasting us for days. They have us completely surrounded.
Yes, and we're running dangerously low on food and ammunition.
I'm not sure how much more we can take, lieutenant colonel.
It's time I talked to the men.
Our fate is sealed. Help is not going to arrive.
cough We'll fight these Mexicans with or without help. *cough*
Well said, Bowie. But know that within a few days—perhaps a few hours— we meet certain doom.

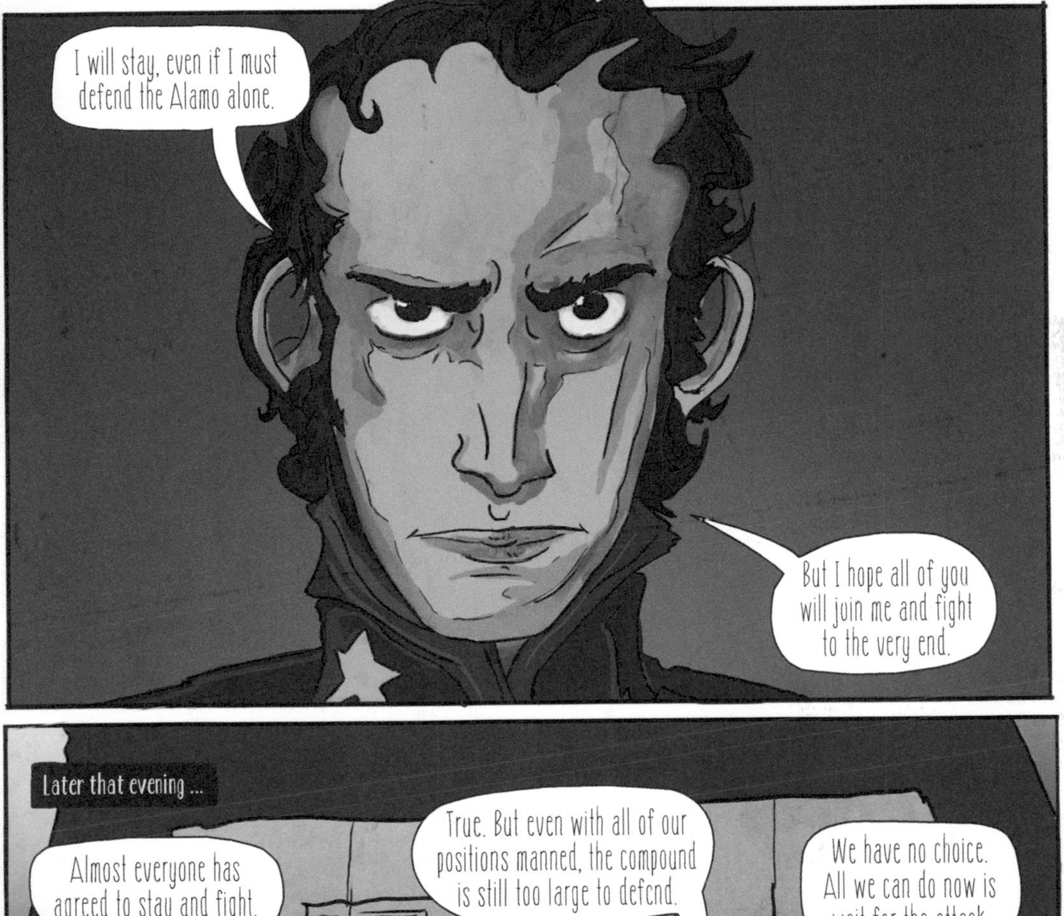
I will stay, even if I must defend the Alamo alone.
But I hope all of you will join me and fight to the very end.
Later that evening ...
Almost everyone has agreed to stay and fight.
True. But even with all of our positions manned, the compound is still too large to defend.
We have no choice. All we can do now is wait for the attack.
ALAM

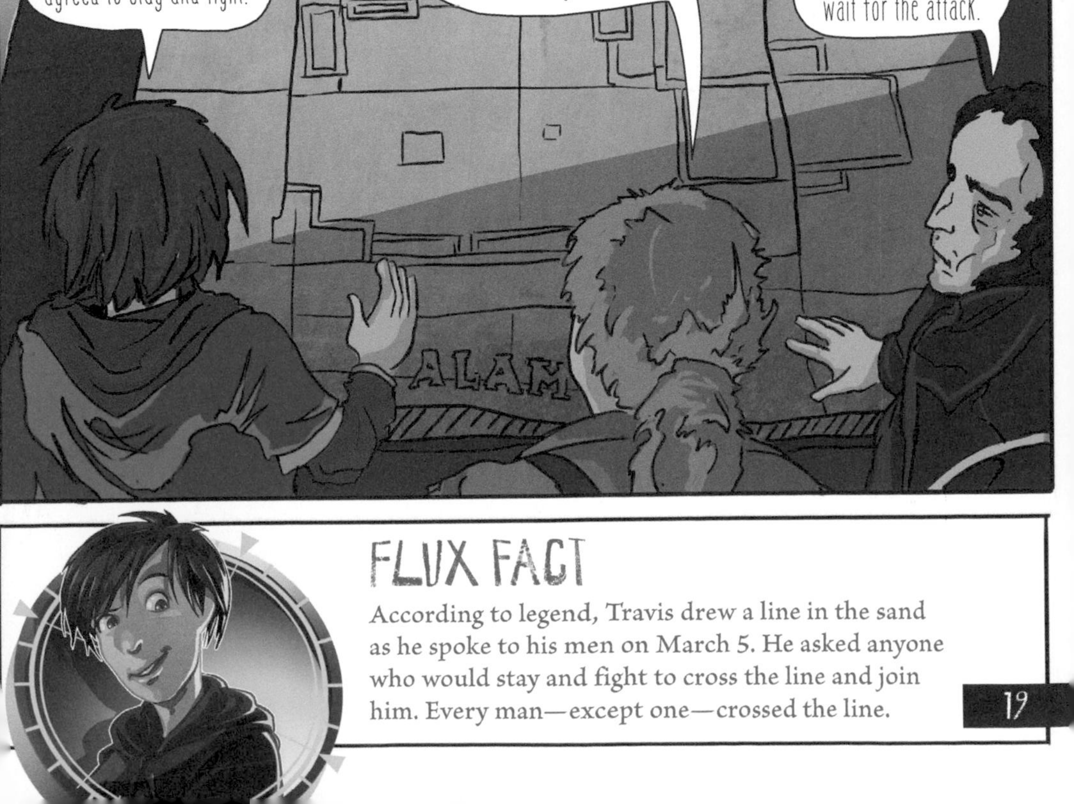

FLUX FACT

According to legend, Travis drew a line in the sand as he spoke to his men on March 5. He asked anyone who would stay and fight to cross the line and join him. Every man—except one—crossed the line.

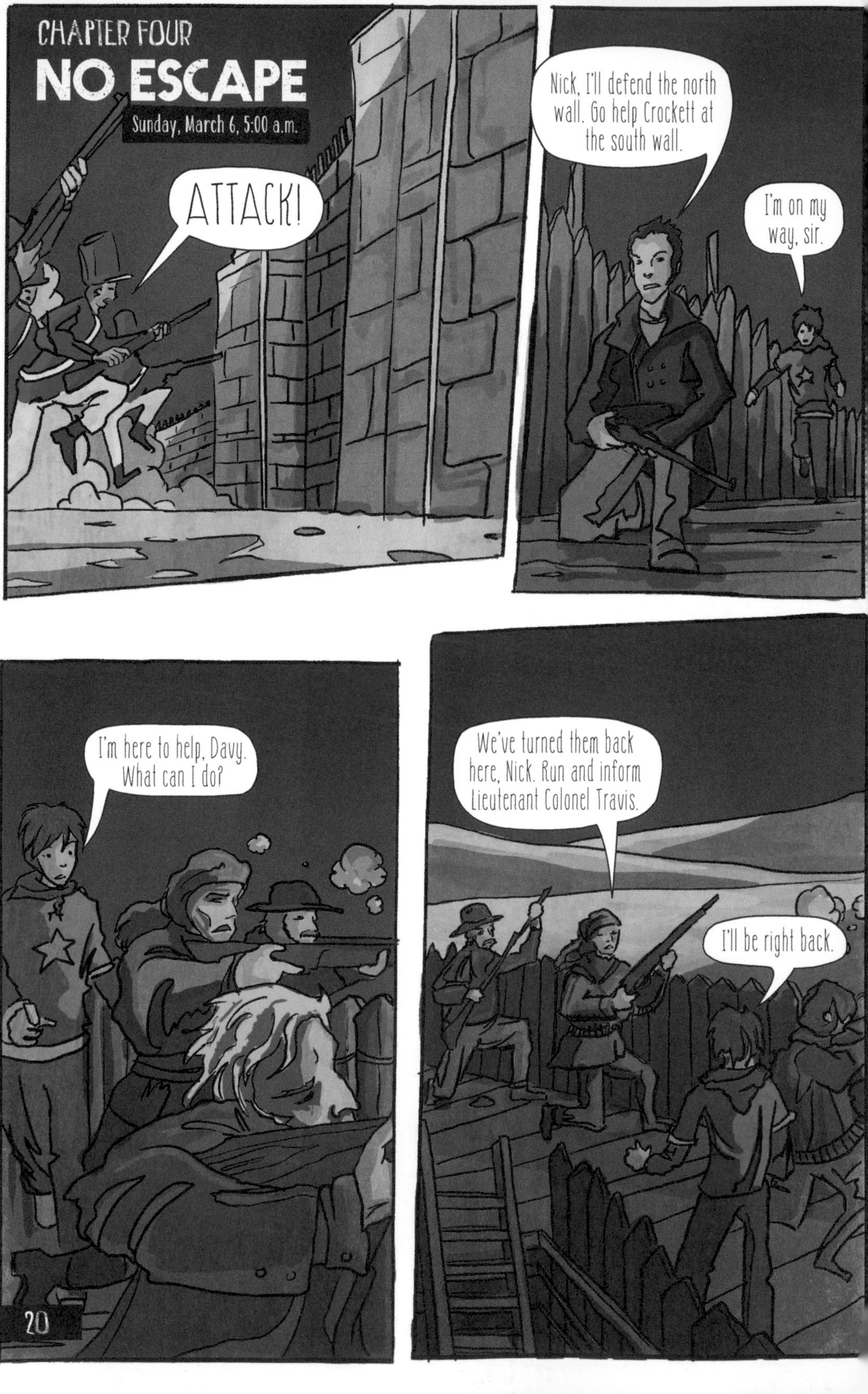
CHAPTER FOUR
NO ESCAPE
Sunday, March 6, 5:00 a.m.
ATTACK!
Nick, I'll defend the north wall. Go help Crockett at the south wall.
I'm on my way, sir.
I'm here to help, Davy. What can I do?
We've turned them back here, Nick. Run and inform Lieutenant Colonel Travis.
I'll be right back.

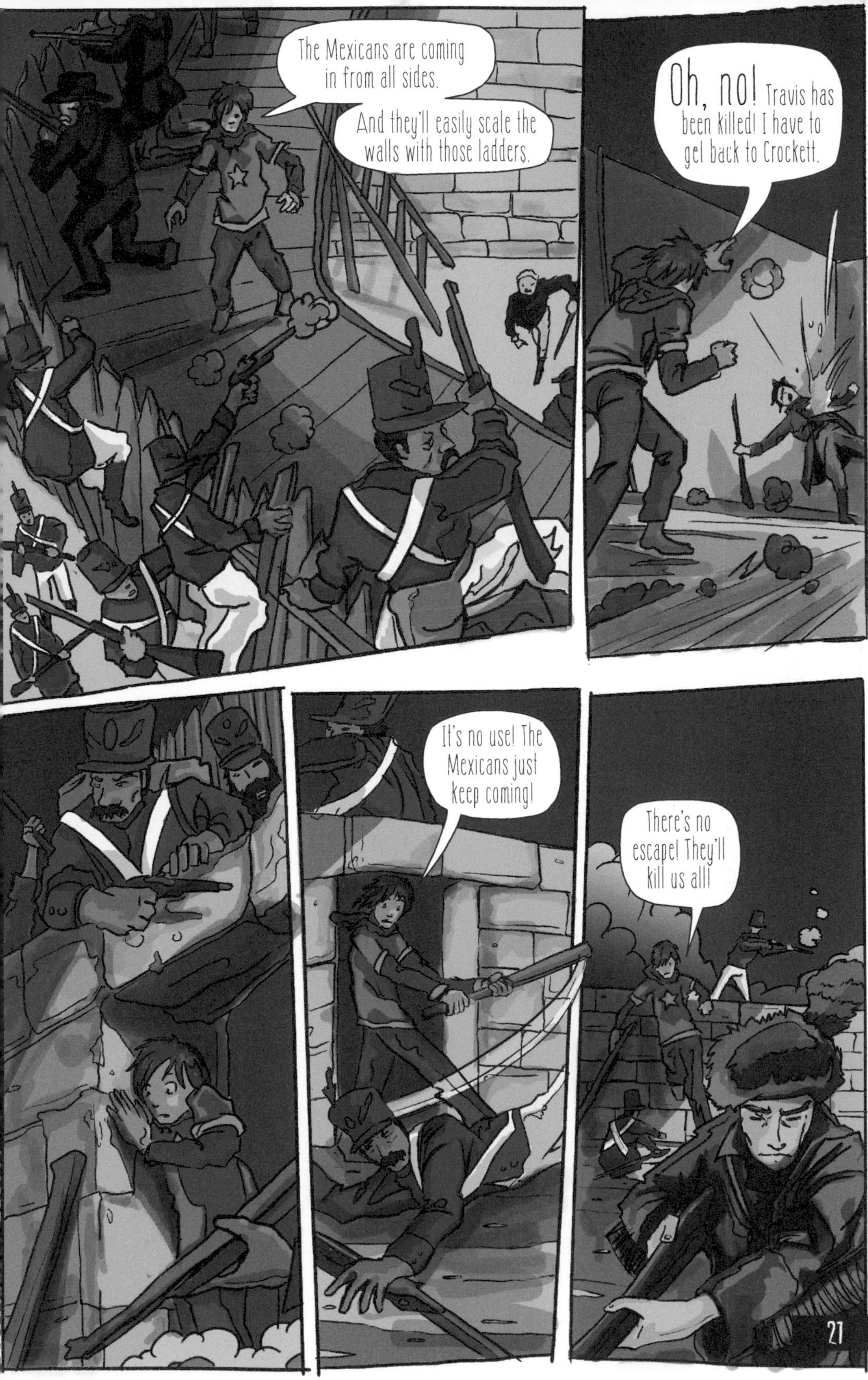
The Mexicans are coming in from all sides.
And they'll easily scale the walls with those ladders.
Oh, no! Travis has been killed! I have to get back to Crockett.
It's no use! The Mexicans just keep coming!
There's no escape! They'll kill us all!

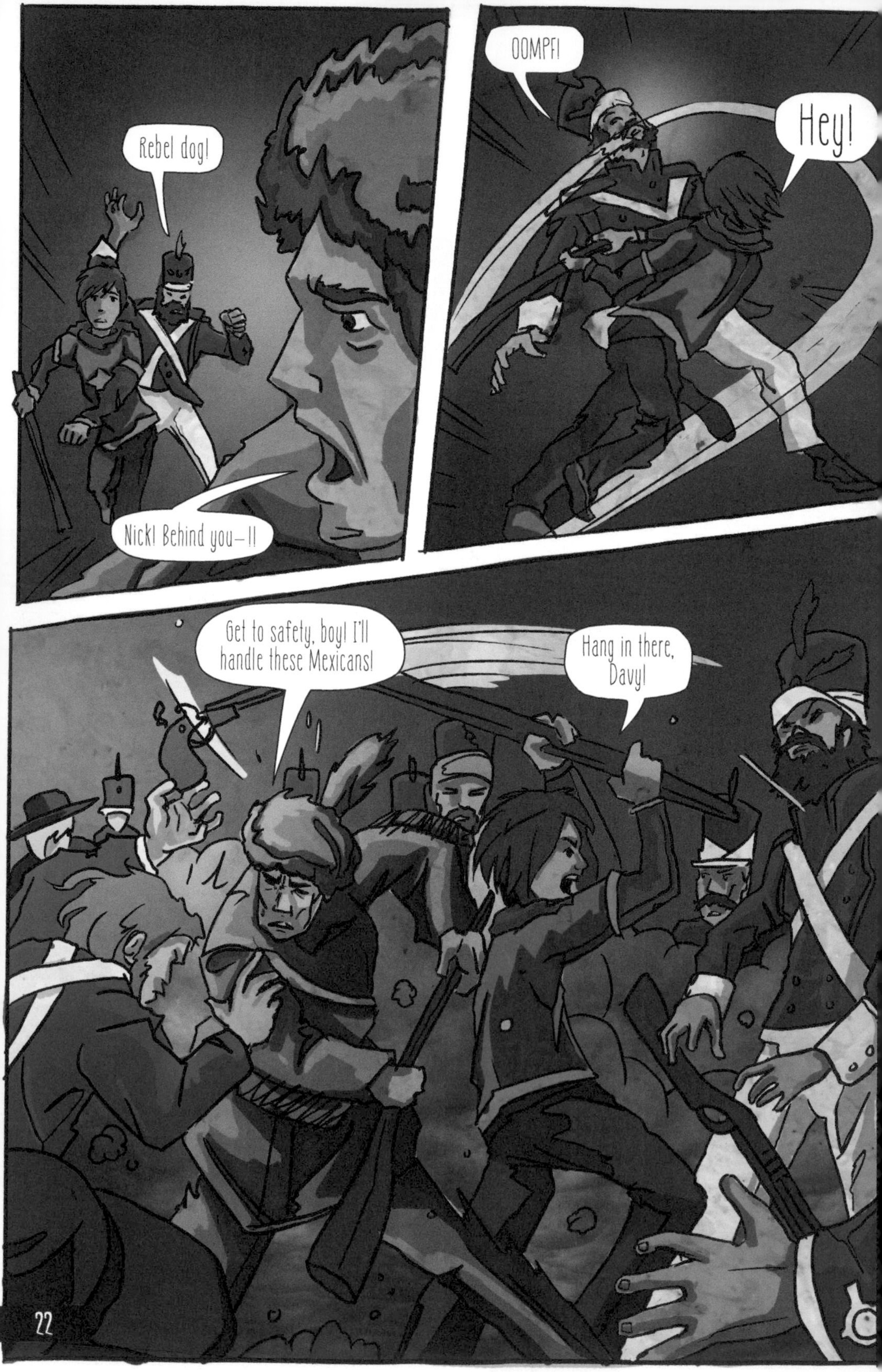
Rebel dog!
Nick! Behind you—!!
OOMPF!
Hey!
Get to safety, boy! I'll handle these Mexicans!
Hang in there, Davy!

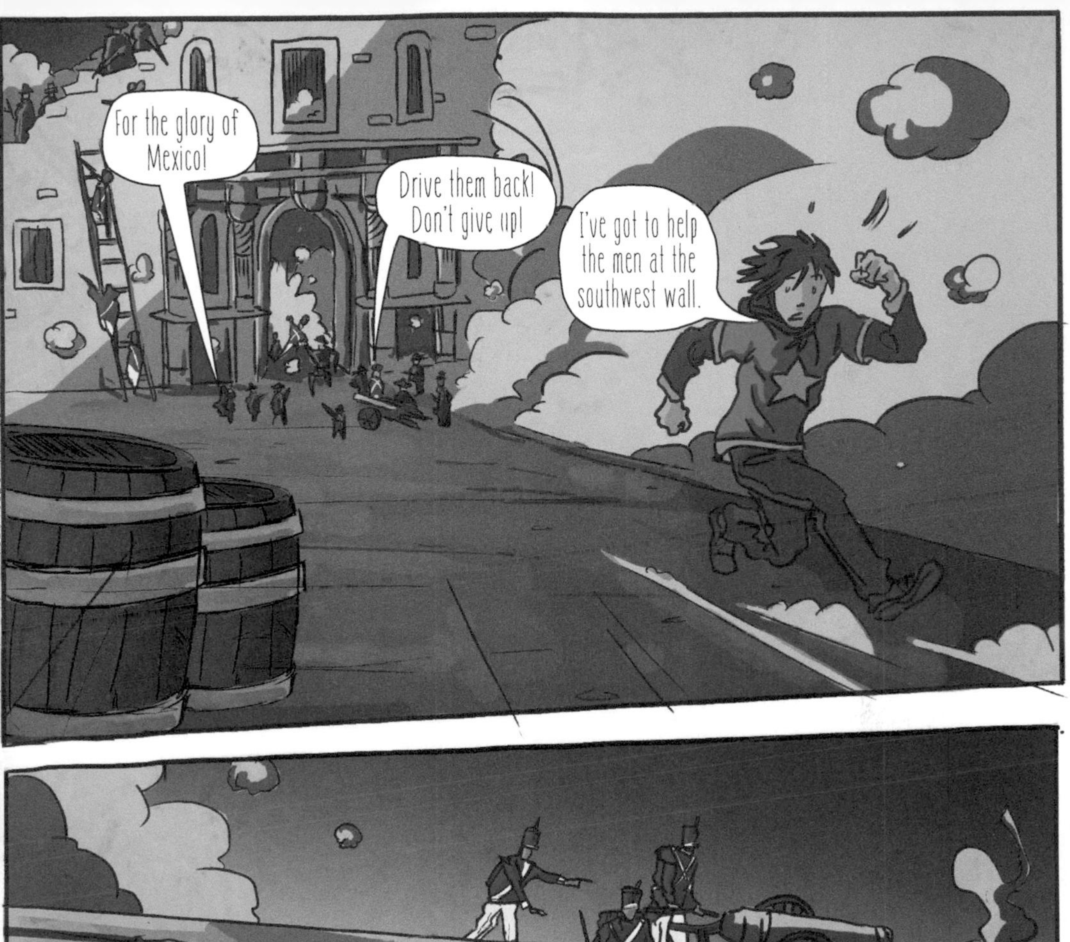
For the glory of Mexico!
Drive them back! Don't give up!
I've got to help the men at the southwest wall.
I'm too late! The Mexicans have taken control of the cannon!
I've got to hide!

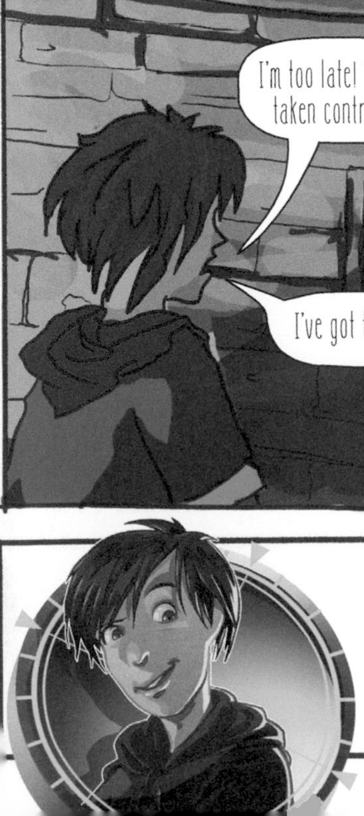

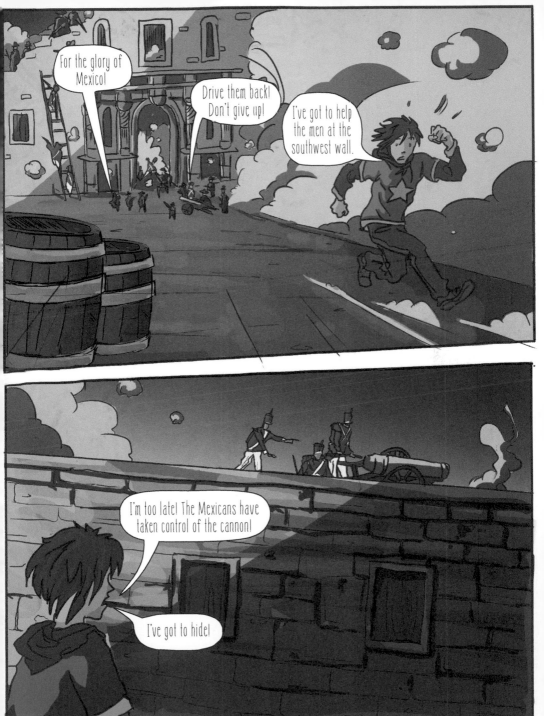

FLUX FACT

The Mexican attackers were packed so tightly together that some of them accidentally shot their fellow soldiers. More Mexicans were killed by "friendly fire" than by the Texian rebels.

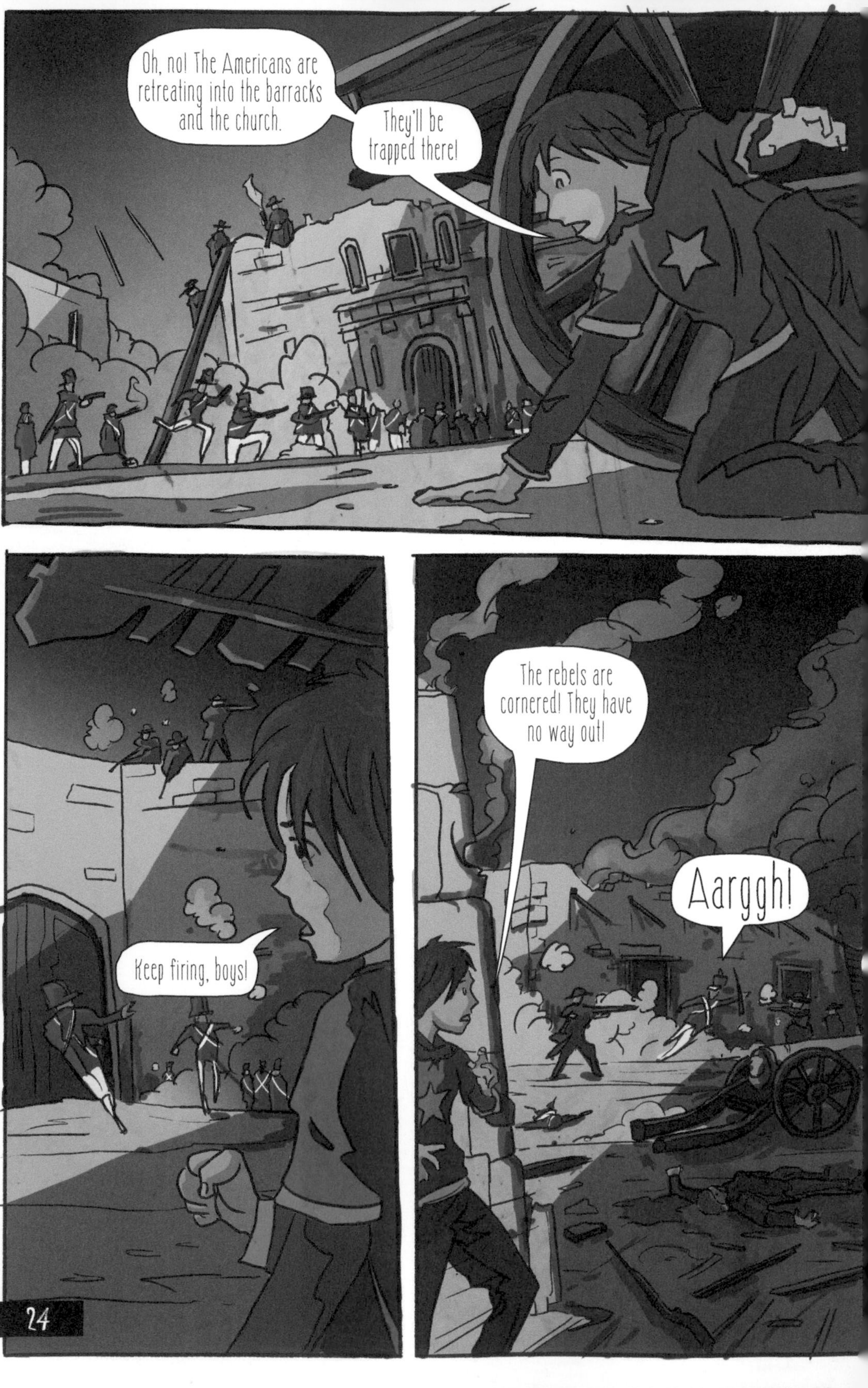
Oh, no! The Americans are retreating into the barracks and the church.
They'll be trapped there!
Keep firing, boys!
The rebels are cornered! They have no way out!
Aargh!

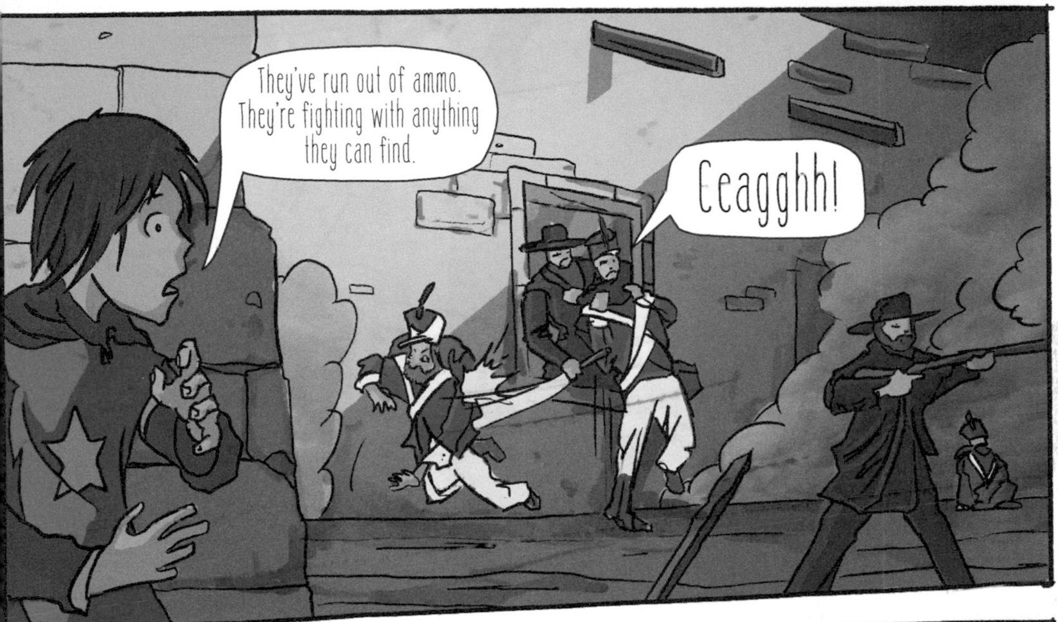
They've run out of ammo. They're fighting with anything they can find.
Ceagghh!

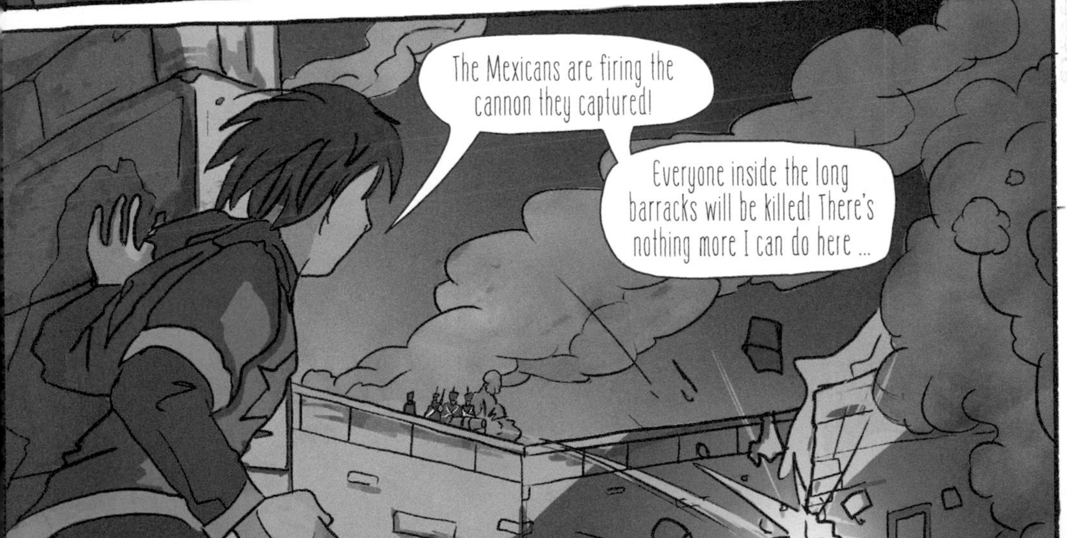
The Mexicans are firing the cannon they captured!
Everyone inside the long barracks will be killed! There's nothing more I can do here ...

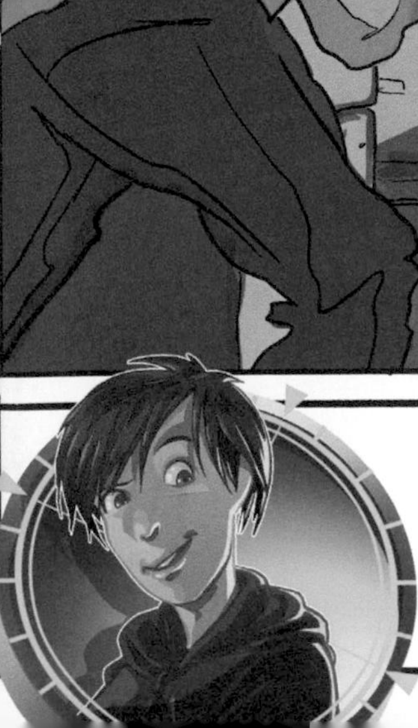

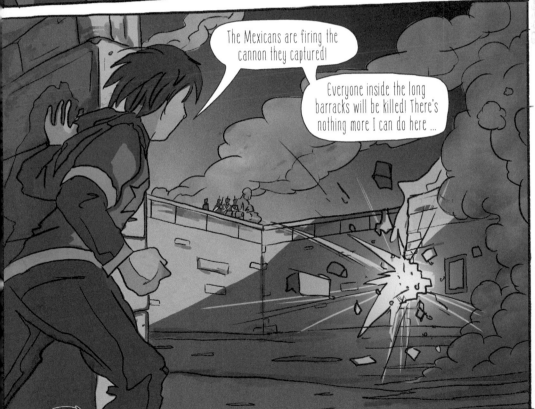

FLUX FACT

Davy Crockett was killed in the fighting. To this day no one is certain how he died. Some historians claim he was killed in the barracks. Others believe he surrendered and was executed after the fighting ended.

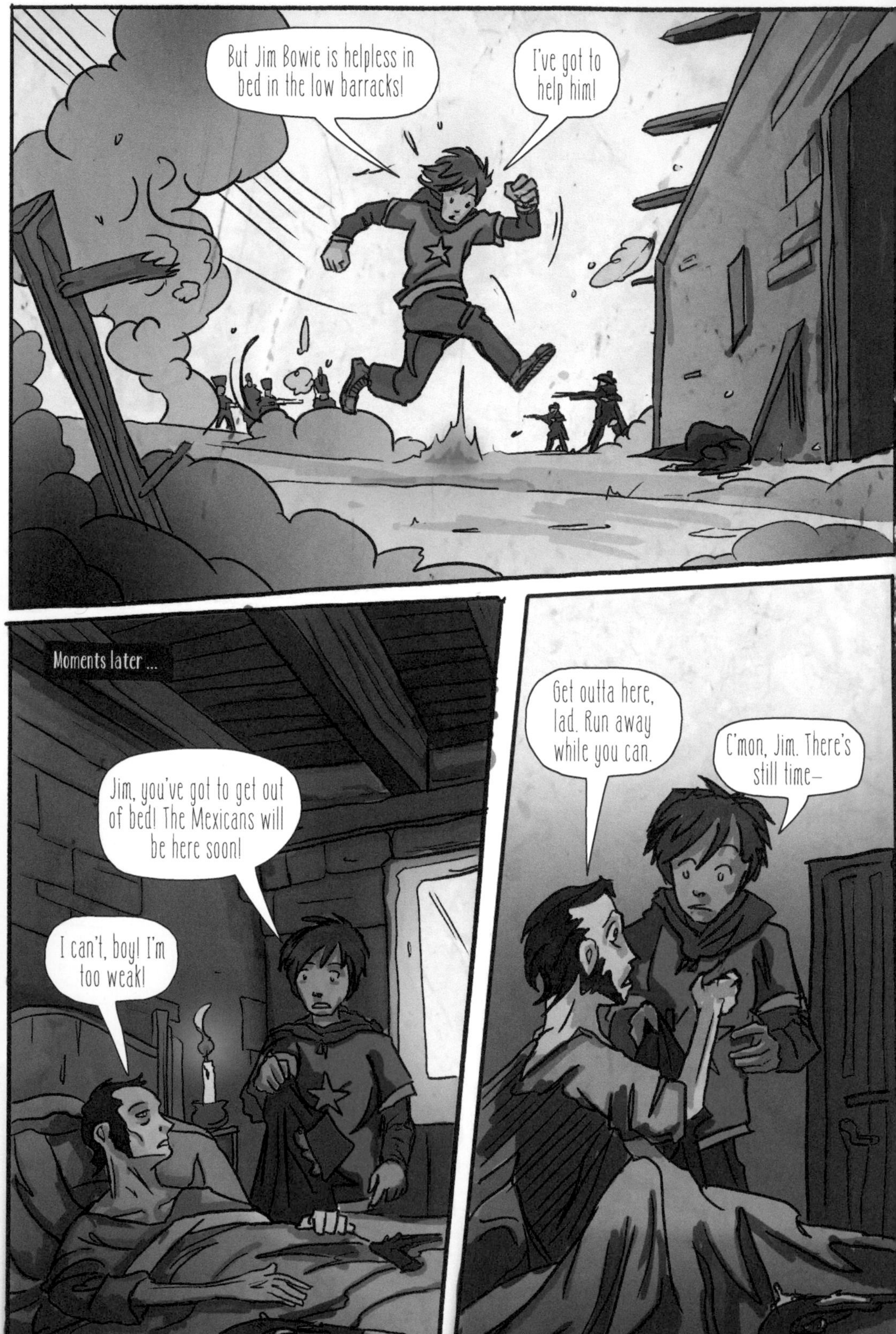

But Jim Bowie is helpless in bed in the low barracks!
I've got to help him!
Moments later ...
Jim, you've got to get out of bed! The Mexicans will be here soon!
I can't, boy! I'm too weak!
Get outta here, lad. Run away while you can.
C'mon, Jim. There's still time—

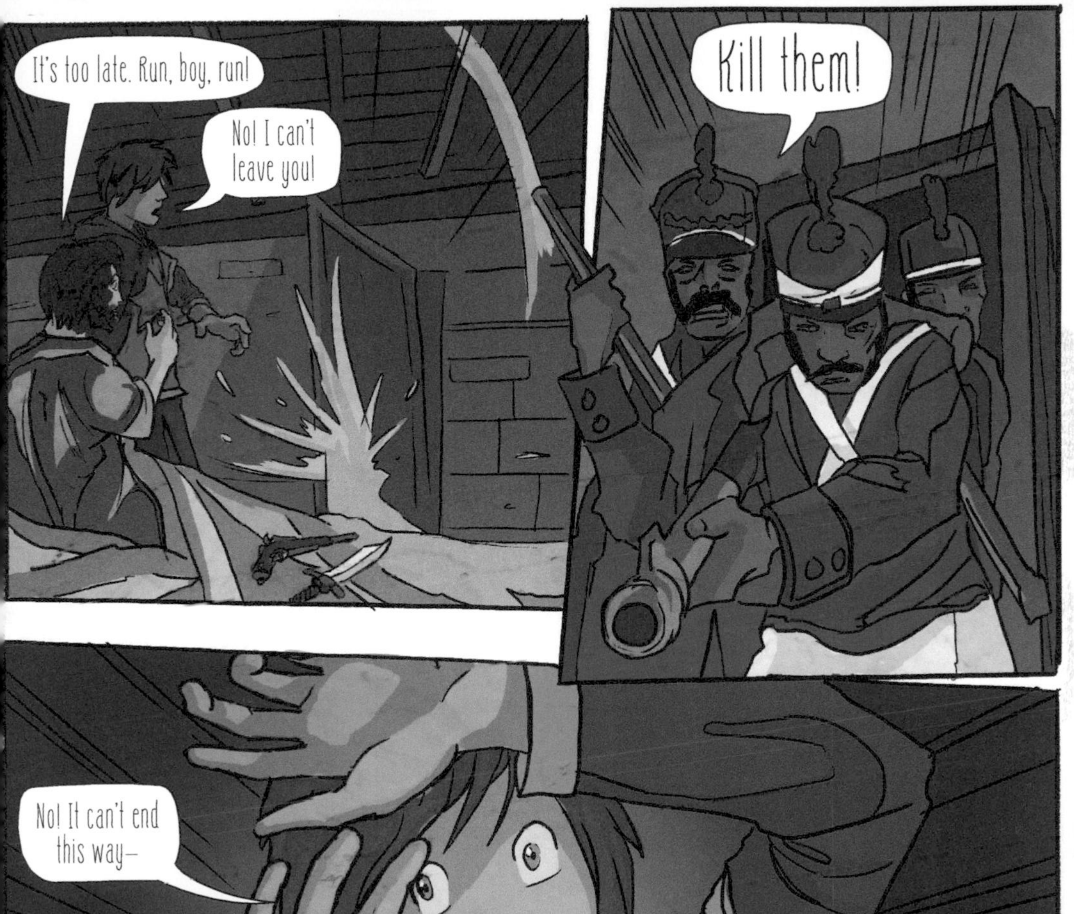
It's too late. Run, boy, run!
No! I can't leave you!
Kill them!
No! It can't end this way–
FZZZZT!

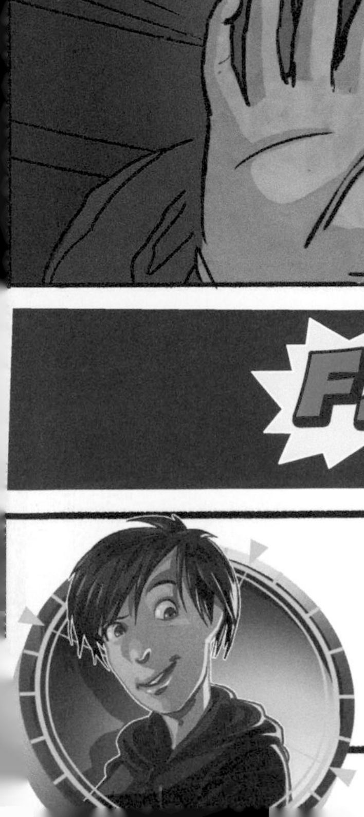

FLUX FACT

Santa Anna ordered his soldiers to take no prisoners. However, the general did spare all the women and children at the Alamo. About 20 were allowed to return to their homes.

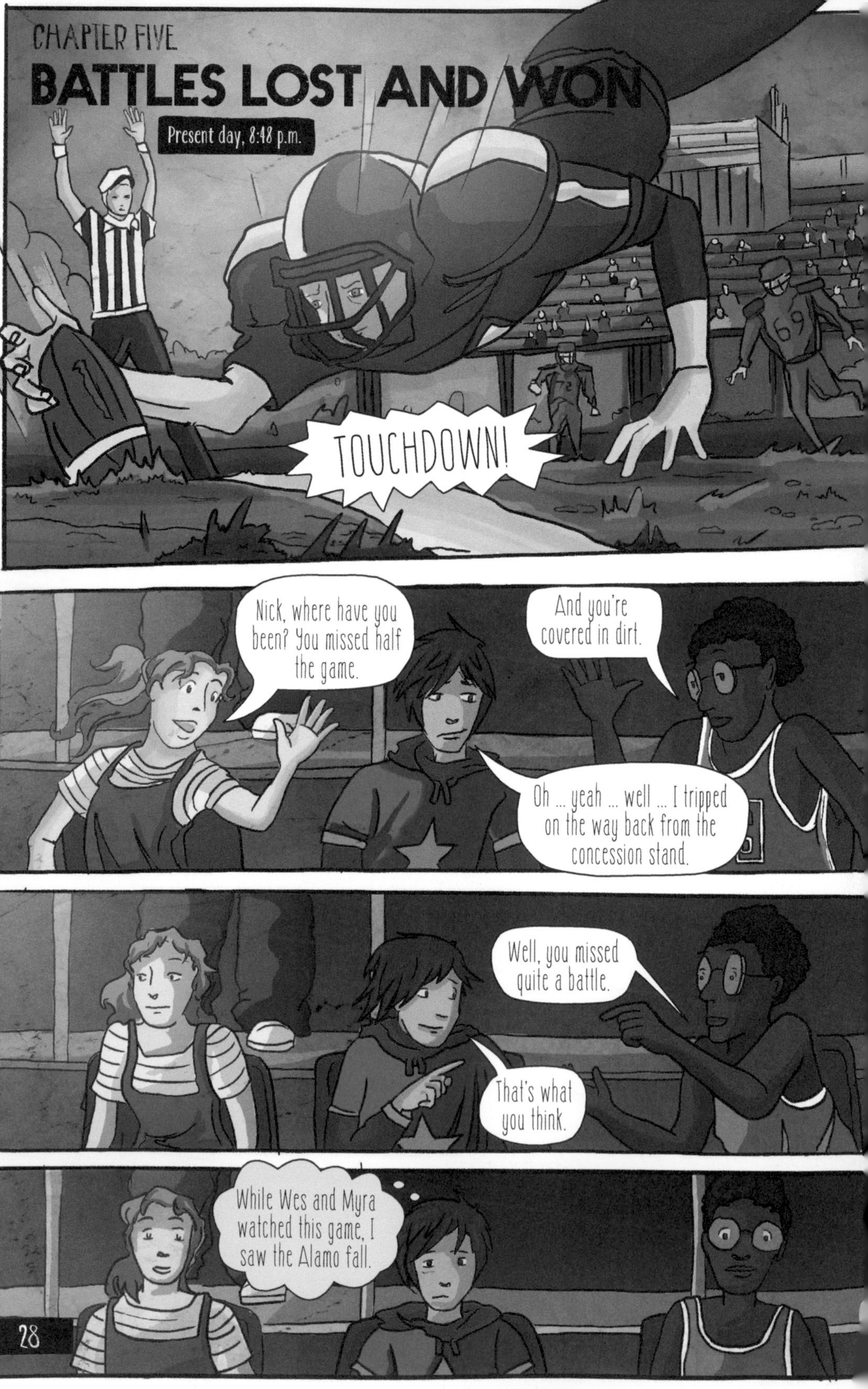
CHAPTER FIVE
BATTLES LOST AND WON
Present day, 8:48 p.m.
TOUCHDOWN!
Nick, where have you been? You missed half the game.
And you're covered in dirt.
Oh ... yeah ... well ... I tripped on the way back from the concession stand.
Well, you missed quite a battle.
That's what you think.
While Wes and Myra watched this game, I saw the Alamo fall.

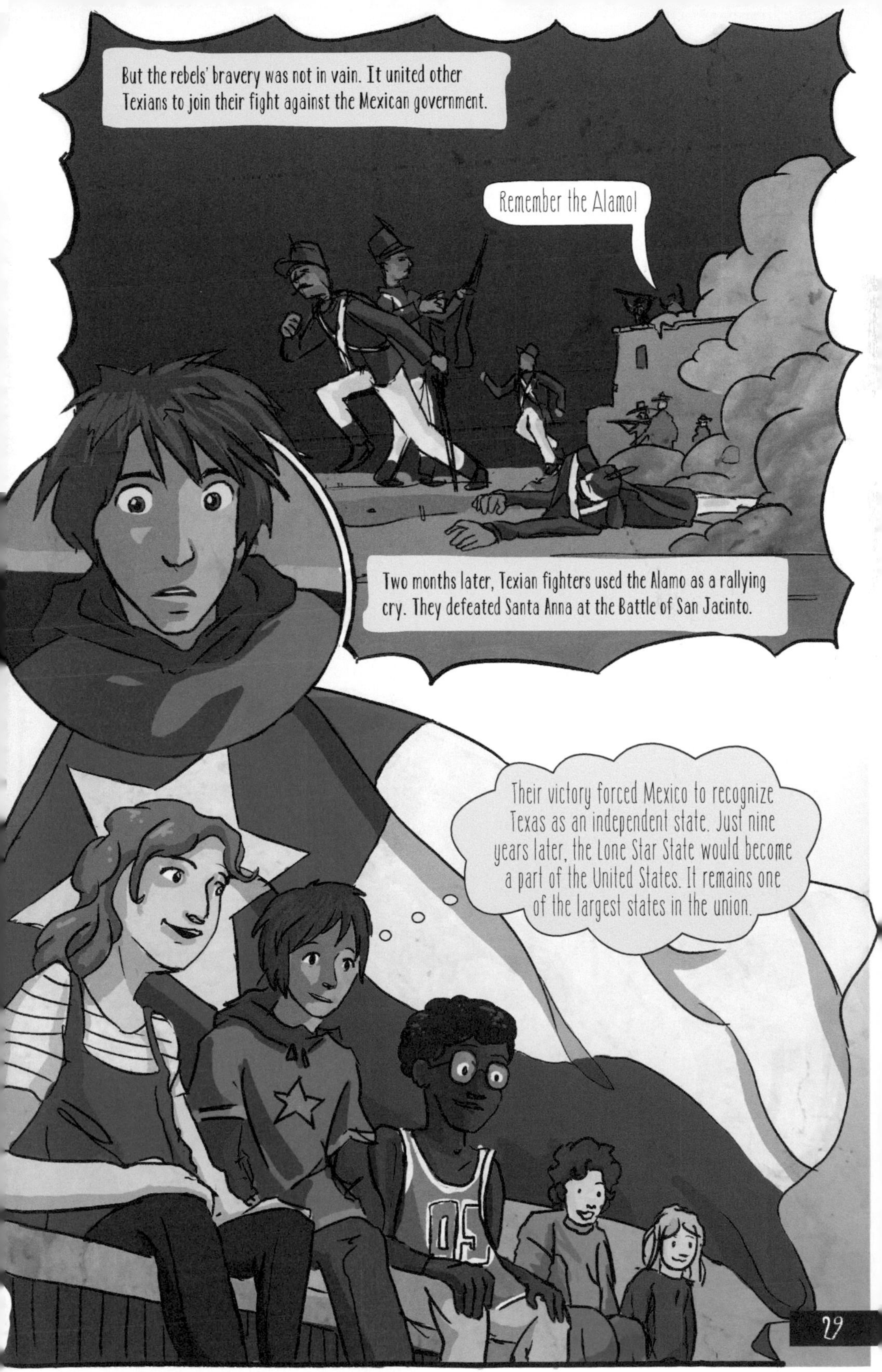

But the rebels' bravery was not in vain. It united other Texians to join their fight against the Mexican government.
Remember the Alamo!
Two months later, Texian fighters used the Alamo as a rallying cry. They defeated Santa Anna at the Battle of San Jacinto.
Their victory forced Mexico to recognize Texas as an independent state. Just nine years later, the Lone Star State would become a part of the United States. It remains one of the largest states in the union.
05

FLUX FILES

TEXAS TERRITORY

Mexico won its independence from Spain in 1821. Texas became a territory within the new nation of Mexico. Texas was one-third the size of the United States at that time.

SPANISH MISSION

The Alamo was originally called San Antonio de Valero. It was a mission built by the Spanish government and used by the Catholic Church. In about 1803, it became a fortress for the Mexican Army. The word alamo means "cottonwood tree" in Spanish.

FIGHTING FOR INDEPENDENCE

Texian settlers believed the Mexican government's policies were harsh toward them. In 1830, the government passed laws to stop American immigration into Texas. In 1833, Santa Anna denied the settlers' request to establish an independent state in Mexico. Doing so would have allowed the settlers to make their own laws and govern themselves. The settlers' anger eventually lead to armed revolts against the Mexicans.

THE ALAMO SIEGE

Santa Anna's siege of the Alamo lasted 12 days before the final attack. During that time, his army fired about 200 cannonballs into the compound. Not one Texian was injured in the constant shelling.

COWARD OF THE ALAMO

Only one man fled the mission when Lieutenant Colonel Travis asked his men to stay and fight on March 5. Louis "Moses" Rose was later nicknamed the "Coward of the Alamo."

JIM BOWIE

Jim Bowie was killed in his bed. Many historians agree that he died after emptying his pistols into several Mexican soldiers.

LIVES LOST

No one knows the exact number of people who died at the Battle of the Alamo. The Alamo's official list counts 189 defenders who lost their lives. Historians estimate about 600 Mexican soldiers died during the battle.

REMEMBER THE ALAMO!

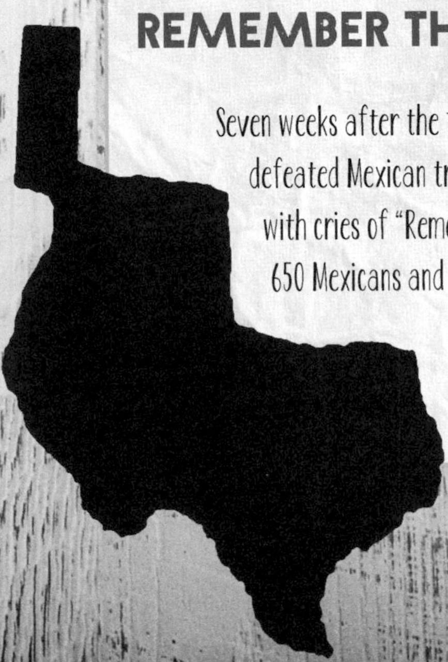

Seven weeks after the fall of the Alamo, an army of rebels defeated Mexican troops at the Battle of San Jacinto. Rallying with cries of "Remember the Alamo!" the Texians killed about 650 Mexicans and captured Santa Anna. Texas became an independent state. In 1845, Texas joined the United States as its 28th state.

GLOSSARY

BARRACKS (BAR-uhks)—the part of a fort where soldiers sleep

COMPOUND (KAHM-paund)—a group of buildings often enclosed by a fence or wall

EXPEDITION (ek-spuh-DISH-uhn)—a journey made for a specific purpose

FORT (FORT)—a building that is well defended against attacks

FORTIFIED (FOR-tuh-fyed)—having had walls built for protection from attack

FRONTIER (fruhn-TEER)—the far edge of a settled area, where few people live

MISSION (MISH-uhn)—a church or other place where missionaries live and work

PIONEER (pye-uh-NEER)—someone who moves to live in a new land

REBEL (REB-uhl)—a person who opposes a government or ruler

SHARPSHOOTER (SHARP-shoo-tur)—someone skilled at hitting small or distant targets

SIEGE (SEEJ)—an attack designed to surround a place and cut it off from supplies and help

SURRENDER (suh-REN-dur)—to give up or admit defeat

READ MORE

JEFFREY, GARY. *The Battle of the Alamo.* A Graphic History of the American West. New York. Gareth Stevens Pub., 2012.

LANDAU, ELAINE. *The Alamo: Would You Join the Fight?* What Would You Do? Berkeley Heights, N.J.: Enslow Publishers Inc., 2014.

SOUTH, VICTOR. *Remember the Alamo: Americans Fight for Texas, 1820–1845.* How America Became America. Philadelphia: Mason Crest Publishers, 2013.

INTERNET SITES

FactHound offers a safe, fun way to find Internet sites related to this book. All sites on FactHound have been researched by our staff.

Here's all you do:

Visit *www.facthound.com*

Type in this code: 9781476539454

Super-cool stuff!

Check out projects, games and lots more at
www.capstonekids.com

INDEX

ABOUT THE AUTHOR

Nel Yomtov is a writer of children's nonfiction books and graphic novels. He specializes in writing about history, country studies, science, and biography. His graphic novel adaptation, *Jason and the Golden Fleece*, published by Stone Arch Books, was a winner of the 2009 Moonbeam Children's Book Award and the 2011 Lighthouse Literature Award. Nel is an avid American military history buff and has written two additional graphic novels for Capstone, *True Stories of World War I* and *True Stories of the Civil War*. He lives in the New York City area.

MORE NICKOLAS FLUX ADVENTURES

ARRESTED FOR WITCHCRAFT!
NICKOLAS FLUX
AND THE SALEM WITCH TRIALS

DEFEND UNTIL DEATH!
NICKOLAS FLUX
AND THE BATTLE OF THE ALAMO

Night of Rebellion!
NICKOLAS FLUX
AND THE BOSTON TEA PARTY

STAKE A CLAIM!
NICKOLAS FLUX
AND THE CALIFORNIA GOLD RUSH

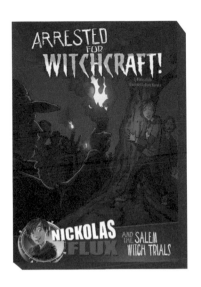

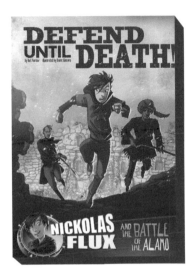

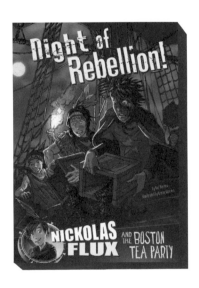

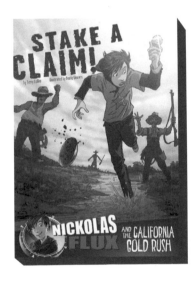